ZEN
BUDDHISM

ZEN
BUDDHISM

*Your Personal Guide
to Practice and Tradition*

JOSHUA R. PASZKIEWICZ

WELLFLEET
PRESS

CONTENTS

INTRODUCTION

Zen Buddhism occupies a unique space among the world's great religions. Technically a school within a school of Buddhist thought, the Zen tradition is essentially an umbrella that covers an array of sects found in Chinese, Korean, Japanese, Vietnamese, and, increasingly, Western cultural contexts. While most Zen orders and sects are remarkably similar when it comes to the essence of their worldviews and training methods, there is also a surprising amount of diversity to be found in the exacting manners in which various traditions seek to apply their practice, in pursuit of the ultimate state of being, known as *awakening*, or enlightenment.

Among the thousands of qualified Zen teachers and lineage holders worldwide, one may find Christian monks and priests, Jewish rabbis, Sufi teachers, and other clerics from major religious traditions. Beyond these and the solely Buddhist adherents of the Zen way, atheists, other self-avowed non-religious folks, and lay people of all stripes can be counted among the senior voices of the broader Zen tradition. Perhaps no other spiritual path in history has enjoyed such widespread intermingling and internal diversity as Zen Buddhism. One might wonder, then: What of substance could a spiritual tradition as seemingly flexible and wide open as Zen have to offer? What tenets and wisdom might Zen possess that make it so attractive to such a diverse array of practitioners? What Zen teachings have enough gravity to religious and non-religious people alike that they could bridge the gap between them? These questions and more are what this book endeavors to answer.

While no single publication can comprehensively address any religious tradition's fullness, this becomes an incredibly challenging task with a subject like Zen Buddhism. Not only is Zen decentralized, but it is also a widespread spiritual tradition that owes its genesis to generations of successive ancestors who are often as much continuers as reformers. Beyond this, the Zen school does not easily trace its origin story back to the charismatic life or ecstatic experience of any one historical founder (beyond the essential teachings of Shakyamuni Buddha that are common to the broader Buddhist religion), making it somewhat hard to pin down. Nonetheless, essential themes and suppositions can be identified and explained.

In the following chapters, this text will examine the history and development of Zen by reviewing the origins of the Buddhist religion itself. Focusing on the fundamental tenets of Buddhism that spread from India into China, where Zen found its birth as the Chan school, we will examine how the Zen tradition developed into a unique vein of Buddhist thought and practice. Growing out of an examination of these essentials, we will then consider in some depth the actual practices that commonly comprise the study of the Zen way, from seated meditation and contemplative practices (like walking meditation, bowing, and working practice) to the nature of spiritual direction and working with a teacher in the Zen school. A whole chapter is then dedicated to the often mysteriously described *koan*, or the case-study examination and practice that Zen is perhaps most well-known for. Throughout the text, we will also devote time to exploring the ongoing dialogue Zen has had with other religious traditions and various secular pursuits, such as the mindfulness movement and various schools of psychotherapy.

It should be noted that every school of Zen Buddhism boldly clings to the central teacher–student relationship as the lynchpin upon which all practice and progression along the Zen path turns. Unfortunately, a book, even of the highest quality, cannot occupy the role of a Zen master. However, any fledgling practitioner or aspiring student of the Zen way would benefit from digesting a comprehensive survey of the history, development, philosophy, and practice of the tradition, beyond the idiosyncratic suppositions that might inform any particular order or sect and its teachers. To paraphrase the famed founding scholar of the discipline of religious studies, Max Müller: when it comes to religion, they who know only one know none!

Keeping this in mind, many Zen adepts, practitioners who are deep into the study, have begun traversing the Zen path with books alone. Of those, a number began with what are now considered relatively poor guides to Zen in literary form. The tenets of sincerity and integrity are most important in setting foot to any spiritual practice. With those values firmly in tow, this book can provide a solid basis for exploring Zen teaching and training and, should a karmic affinity with the tradition become apparent, it can guide the sincere seeker in taking the next steps in an informed and responsible way.

Finally, while this text primarily utilizes Japanese terms in exploring the Zen tradition, it is not a book focused on the Japanese Zen schools exclusively. In the Western world, Japanese Zen was the first iteration of Zen Buddhism to arrive and capture the attention of its students and writers. Therefore, in the English-speaking world, Zen is best known through Japanese-aligned terminology, with teachers of Chinese, Korean, and Vietnamese import often using such terms for familiarity and simplicity. In the following chapters, Zen will be explored with broad respect to each of the original cultures that have inherited and birthed Zen traditions, in every way except language.

The general nature of the emerging Western Zen tradition in the English-speaking world is a blend of various influences. Indeed, there is hardly a teacher authorized in any bona fide lineage—regardless of the cultural container of the particular sect—that hasn't been influenced in some way by the teachings of Vietnamese Zen master Thich Nhat Hanh, for instance, or those of the Japanese master Shunryu Suzuki, or the Korean master Seung Sahn. This book bows in deference to the teachings of each legitimate Zen school, holding none above any other, and in doing so seeks to allow you, the reader, to lean into what naturally attracts you as you pursue further study or training in the Zen way.

While this text is not a how-to manual per se, it is strewn with invitations to move from mere thinking about Zen to experiencing it by applying the various principles, teachings, and practices explored in the context of your daily life through guided meditations and exercises.

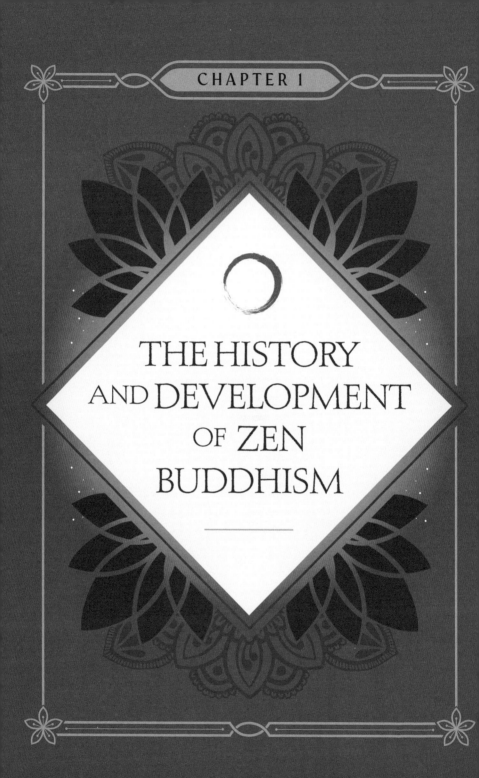

CHAPTER 1

THE HISTORY AND DEVELOPMENT OF ZEN BUDDHISM

One cannot begin to understand Zen without first grasping its foundation, Buddhism. Despite contemporary attempts to untie Zen from Buddhism, the fact remains (as the title of this book attests) that Zen is part and parcel of Buddhism. So, what then is Buddhism? For many in the West, Buddhism is best known as the religion seemingly propagated by the jolly gentleman portrayed in statues adorning the counter of many Asian restaurants and establishments. Perhaps the word *Buddhism* invokes vague images of saffron-vested, head-shorn monks. To the more informed, Buddhism might be cast as "more of a way of life than a religion," a life that is all about peace and good vibes, sans the problematic doctrines and dogmas that have informed the socio-political confrontations of the modern day. None of these images or allusions, however, are quite right. In this chapter, we'll explore the history and tenets of Buddhism, and where this thing called *Zen* might fit into it and them.

SIDDHARTHA GAUTAMA

The history of the Buddhist religion stretches back some 2,500 years to the Indus River Valley, in an area known to the contemporary world as Nepal. There, in the ancient city of Lumbini, a boy named Siddhartha Gautama was born to the chieftain of the Shakya clan, heir apparent to his father's throne. It is said in the hagiography of the Buddhist tradition (stories meant to point to truth) that it was prophesied around the young Siddhartha's birth that the boy was destined to follow one of two paths: either assuming his father's rule as successor or, in renouncing his birthright as a spiritual seeker, becoming a world-renowned sage. Naturally, Siddhartha's father was invested in the wellbeing of his people and thus the continuance of his rule. He is said to have done everything in his power to groom his son as his heir while trying to dissuade him from becoming too interested in spiritual matters.

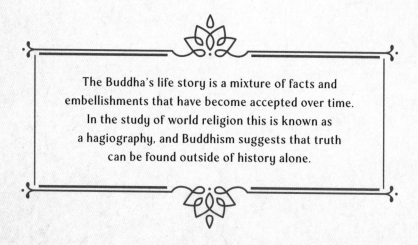

The Buddha's life story is a mixture of facts and embellishments that have become accepted over time. In the study of world religion this is known as a hagiography, and Buddhism suggests that truth can be found outside of history alone.

The young Siddhartha Gautama was raised in quite a sheltered manner. Relegated to private princely dwellings, among all the earthly and sensual pleasures that wealth and privilege could provide, Siddhartha rarely ventured from his closely curated domicile. However, successful as this setting was in suppressing the existential yearnings that underpin most spiritual quests, it was inadequate preparation for a young prince set to assume his father's role as leader of his people. Eventually, Siddhartha would have to be introduced to the wider world so that he might come to know his people, and in knowing them might earn their loyalty and trust. To these ends, Siddhartha's father arranged for an appropriate introduction to the wider chiefdom at a fall festival as the boy neared his coming of age. Alas, in finally meeting the wider world, Siddhartha was forced squarely onto the razor's edge of the prophecy concerning his life direction. Indeed, he was confronted for the first time with four sights that would ignite a disarming sense of alarm concerning his lack of understanding of the wider world and his place within it.

Leaving the confines of his lavish and protected abode, the young Siddhartha quickly came to behold elderly people, sick people, and even a dead body for the first time. The forces of old age, sickness, and death weighed heavily on Siddhartha's mind. When the boy met a wandering ascetic—a person who lives by a strict set of religious rules—he encountered the notion of seeking to understand life amidst these realities. With this, Siddhartha's fate was essentially sealed. In short order, the young prince was destined to renounce his inheritance, and his life entirely as he had known it, and he set out from the confines of his home to become a perpetual wanderer and spiritual seeker.

The ascetic Gautama, as he would come to be called, sought far and wide for the meaning of and answers to life's quandaries as he had quickly come to know them. He studied with esteemed teachers, debated with and bested prominent pundits, and practiced austerities with such fervor that his body would be forced to the brink of death. Finally, as none of these endeavors brought about any real or lasting resolution to his questions, Siddhartha withdrew into himself, sitting in quiet contemplation beneath a banyan tree, where he vowed to awaken to liberating spiritual insight or die trying. As fate would have it, after some time the ascetic Gautama did indeed realize the enlightenment that he had so sought, and with his mind finally at ease, he would begin teaching and become known as the Buddha: The Awakened One.

WORLDVIEWS IN THE BUDDHA'S ERA

The prevailing worldview of the Buddha's time was essentially a form of proto-Hinduism. This spiritual schema put forward the concept that sentient lifeforms are first and foremost spiritual beings, not bodies. Instead, material bodies were vessels piloted by souls in their experience of material consciousness. This material consciousness is problematic, though, as it is separate from the actual dwelling place of souls. Souls are meant to be in union with the supreme, impersonal, creative potency of the universe, or God.

The mechanism by which souls could separate from God and incarnate into physical bodies on a material plane is quite complex, but suffice it to say, once a soul finds itself on the other side of the dividing line between impersonal absorption in the Godhead and individual experience in the material world, one must play by those rules. It seems that the laws of the material universe manifest chiefly as time and complex chains of cause-and-effect known as *karma-vipaka*, which ultimately result in an unsatisfactory cycle of migratory lifetimes. Time and time again, the soul at the death of the body would, according to karmic circumstance, either migrate toward higher planes of existence or lower planes of existence, on a cosmic journey toward (or away from) reconciliation and thus union with the Godhead.

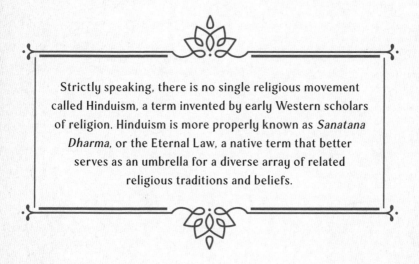

Strictly speaking, there is no single religious movement called Hinduism, a term invented by early Western scholars of religion. Hinduism is more properly known as *Sanatana Dharma*, or the Eternal Law, a native term that better serves as an umbrella for a diverse array of related religious traditions and beliefs.

Within this environment, the Buddha cultivated ultimately unsatisfactory spiritual insights, trying as he might to track down his true nature as a spirit-self, so much so that the material body might be cast off at death, and along with it, material consciousness. That spirit-self, though, never seemed to materialize for the ascetic Gautama, and upon his awakening, he would declare that no such thing could be found. With this postulation, he would disrupt the whole of the prevailing spiritual worldview of his time and begin a new way.

BUDDHA'S NEW WAY

The new way that we today call Buddhism, begun by Siddhartha, the sage of the Shakya clan, offered a revised worldview to its adherents. Instead of focusing on a mysterious journey toward reunion with a supreme god, it focused on observable reality, and then only on those things that could be confidently known to help the human condition. The Buddha was chiefly concerned with the very nature of suffering and the causes and conditions of its cessation. He articulated this concern in a teaching we know today as the Four Noble Truths.

The Four Noble Truths is both a simple and profound teaching that is universally revered by Buddhists around the globe. Essentially comprised of four words—namely *Dukkha* (Suffering), *Samudaya* (Arising), *Nirodha* (Cessation), and *Marga* (Path), when expounded upon, these words portray a sophisticated understanding of the human condition, its pitfalls, and a way through them.

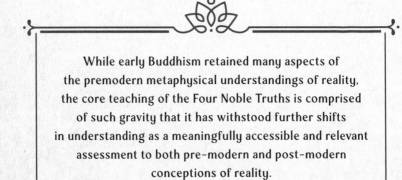

While early Buddhism retained many aspects of the premodern metaphysical understandings of reality, the core teaching of the Four Noble Truths is comprised of such gravity that it has withstood further shifts in understanding as a meaningfully accessible and relevant assessment to both pre-modern and post-modern conceptions of reality.

DUKKHA

Dukkha, commonly translated to mean suffering, is perhaps better understood as unsatisfactory-ness. Applied to the whole of human experience, the word means "a wheel that binds." In other words, life seems to be demarcated by a sense of dis-ease, wherein no matter how good things are, they could always be a little bit better, or at least they could last a little longer. The concept of Dukkha does not suggest that life does not entail joy or goodness, just that even joy and goodness carry gloomy shadows. To follow the etymology, a cart with four wheels isn't useless or irreparable when it is revealed to have a binding wheel; that bound wheel just makes the cart harder to use and enjoy.

SAMUDAYA

Samudaya, or arising, suggests that the dis-ease of Dukkha is not self-sustaining or primal but that it arises due to specific causes and conditions. Essentially those causes and conditions are impermanence and craving, or desire. Because all things are fundamentally impermanent and in transition, they tend to be dissatisfying when we treat them as if they were any other way. In this, desiring or craving for things to be any other way than the way that they are is also a source of dissatisfaction and suffering.

NIRODHA

Nirodha, or cessation, provides hope for the sentient state. The very possibility of the cessation of Dukkha (that is, suffering) is a lamp lit from Samudaya (the arising of Dukkha from conditions). Because suffering arises from specific causes and conditions, those causes and conditions themselves may be addressed and thereby bring about an end to suffering.

MARGA

Finally, there is Marga, the path toward the cessation of suffering. Just as suffering arises from specific causes and conditions, so too does cessation unfold from its own causes and conditions. In the case of Marga, the Buddha illustrated what is called the Noble Eightfold Path of right view, intention, speech, action, livelihood, effort, concentration, and mindfulness. Simply, in seeing things as they are (chiefly, as impermanent and manifest) rather than as they are not and then acting in accord with that perception and understanding, the very process that gives way to the genesis of suffering can be arrested, and indeed cessation can be manifest.

THE BUDDHA'S TEACHINGS AND SCHOOLS OF BUDDHIST THOUGHT

From this basis, in the profound yet clear teaching of the Four Noble Truths, the Buddha Gautama bounded and taught continuously for the rest of his life. Unlike other religions and spiritual leaders who espoused systematic theologies given seemingly once and for all of time, the Buddha taught on an occasional basis—that is, teaching to the occasion in which he found himself. Many of the Buddhist scriptures are essentially recordings of the Buddha's teaching to specific individuals and groups paired with contextual details outlining why and how he came to address them.

For all of the flexibility and potential breadth of occasional philosophy, it does have its limitations. After a long life of teaching, upon his death it became clear to the Buddha's vast body of followers that there were perhaps many questions they had failed to ask their teacher or that had simply never come up. This would rather quickly lead to various schisms and splinters among the Buddha's original body of disciples, who, as time went on, would find themselves divided on any number of issues. Eventually, exemplary teachers, scholars, and apologists would appear, and new schools of Buddhist practice would develop and evolve, spreading outward all the while. In the substantial wake of the Buddha's life and teaching, his followers and the generations of their disciples would essentially coalesce into four identifiable primary schools of thought. The orthodox students who sought to preserve the Buddha's dispensation precisely as it had been given would come to be known as Theravadins (literally, "followers of the way of the elders") and would generally remain in Southeast Asia. The various reformers who sought to adapt the Buddha's teaching to the times and places in which they found themselves, naturally extending and expanding doctrine along the way, would become known as Mahayanists (followers of the greater vehicle) and would spread their teachings into Far East Asia. As the Mahayanists carried their teaching eastward, their interactions with the native religious traditions of the Himalayas (exemplified in places like Bhutan) would give rise to yet another easily identifiable school known as Vajrayana (the "diamond vehicle"). And finally, the Mahayana school in China would eventually give rise to a fourth vehicle, known as Zen.

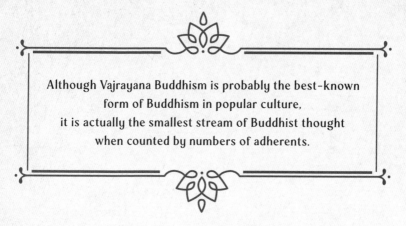

Although Vajrayana Buddhism is probably the best-known
form of Buddhism in popular culture,
it is actually the smallest stream of Buddhist thought
when counted by numbers of adherents.

To make an analogy of Christianity, the Theravada school is easily
comparable to the Roman Catholic and Orthodox churches. In contrast,
the Mahayana school might be understood as a movement akin to the
Protestant Reformation, leaving Vajrayana as a syncretic school that
encompasses more than one school of thought, similar to Santeria, and
Zen as a restorationist movement.

THE ZEN MOVEMENT

To narrow in on Zen specifically, Mahayana Buddhism was already
well established in China, with institutions like the infamous Shaolin
Temple running and primed for the arrival of the quasi-mystic founder
of the Zen tradition Bodhidharma in 527 AD. However, by all reports
in the founding mythos of Zen, the Buddhist training that had been
transplanted to China lacked vitality and vigor. Indeed, Bodhidharma
is said to have found the monks of Shaolin in such poor health (from
hours spent in various modes of lackluster meditation and complex
intellectual pursuits) that both their mental and physical states were

so diminished that the realization of Buddhism's deeper essence was entirely inaccessible to them. As such, Bodhidharma immediately introduced a substantial regime of yogic training exercises at Shaolin that are said to have laid the foundation for the eventual development of systematized martial arts and energy cultivation disciplines such as kung fu and qigong in China. In this, Bodhidharma reestablished a link between body and mind in Buddhist cultivation that continues to play a significant role in defining Zen practice today.

In the preceding paragraphs, Zen was cast as a restoration movement, a school of seeking what the Buddha sought through applying the spirit of what the Buddha taught rather than by enshrining the letters of his context-bound words and vision for all of time. The heart of the Zen way is thus summarized in what is called Bodhidharma's Four Sacred Verses, which define Zen as:

A *special transmission outside of the scriptures;*
Not dependent on words or letters;
Directly pointing to the heart-mind;
Perceiving one's true nature and becoming Buddha.

To break this teaching down a bit, we may understand that essentially Bodhidharma taught that the entire purpose of Buddhist training, as it would be inherited in the Zen school, is to attain the same mind of Buddha and thereby become one with the sage of the Shakya clan, Siddhartha Gautama. To do this, the Buddhist cultivar must seek to perceive themselves and reality directly, understanding that the mind-heart is utterly enmeshed with the very nature of reality. Further, it is through a direct pointing out of this reality, an introduction by way of someone who has clearly perceived it, that is, a relationship with a realized spiritual director, that the cultivar walks in the footsteps of the Buddha. This pointing cannot be contained in words or letters; a mind-to-mind, disciplic transmission in shared presence is simultaneously the key, the door, and the path.

ZEN MASTERS

Because of the limitations of words and letters, that is, their inability to contain the transcendent wisdom that emanates from the experience of awakening, teachers play a central role in the practice of Zen Buddhism. Teachers can relate to their pupils in ways that transcend the strictures of dogmas and doctrines, and through their very presence, and through the occasional spontaneity of their actions and responses, teachers can attune their students' minds to accord with the awakened view of any given situation. Therefore, the whole of one's life and one's shared encounters with the teacher can thus become the source of great potential in the pursuit of awakening.

The centrality of the relationship with a teacher or spiritual director is not unique to Zen among other Buddhist traditions. For instance, in the early Buddhist scripture collection the *Samyutta Nikaya*, a story is recounted wherein Shakyamuni Buddha is traveling with his attendant Ananda. At some point, Ananda addresses the Buddha, and in paraphrase offers a sentiment to the effect of, "Teacher, I think I have finally grasped something of the spiritual life." "What is it, then, Ananda?" inquires the Buddha. Ananda replies, "Spiritual direction, the relationship with the spiritual teacher, is at least half of the spiritual life." To this the Buddha responds in lament, "Say not so, Ananda. Say not so. This spiritual relationship is indeed the whole of the spiritual life!" What we might understand as unique to the Zen tradition is its casting of its spiritual directors and duly qualified teachers as direct spiritual descendants of the Buddha himself through a rite generally known as "dharma transmission". In the dharma transmission rite, the recipient is situated within a spiritual bloodline, typically stretching today through eighty or more generations of names, back to the Buddha, as a Zen master—ideally, an awakened being, whose insight is comparable with that of the Buddha's.

LINEAGE

While Buddhism tends to enjoy a fairly wholesome image and reputation in the contemporary world, it is not immune to the pitfalls of religiosity, politics, and indeed humanity in general. Though Zen tends to place a great emphasis on lineage as a key component in establishing the bona fide status of any given teacher, the reality is that most of every Zen lineage is at least somewhat contrived. As the Zen school was developing in China it faced an upward battle to find acceptance in Chinese culture as something of a new and foreign religion simultaneously. Chinese culture, both at the time of Zen's formation and blossoming as well as today, is one that deeply values history, ancestors, and tradition. It is for this reason that the so-called bloodline lineage of awakened successors of the Buddha came to be developed, seemingly in the Tang dynasty. And while the essence of the common Zen lineage charts speaks toward the real movement and succession of a religious tradition, it ultimately conveys these details both creatively and colorfully.

In the founding mythos of the Zen school, a story is told of a sermon delivered by the Buddha on Vulture Peak to a vast assembly of disciples. In this sermon, the Buddha simply sat wordlessly for a time, the object of his many students' gazes. Finally, the Buddha silently raised a single flower, and one of the senior students present in the assembly, the Venerable Mahakashyapa, understanding the Buddha's intention and meaning, smiled. This action by the Buddha and its receipt by Mahakashyapa is said to be the first instance of dharma transmission in the Zen line, whereby Mahakashyapa became the Buddha's spiritual successor. In reality, though, this story is a fabricated recasting of actual history, told to solidify the Zen lineage and ensure its positive reception within Chinese society, a task it ultimately accomplished.

However, history tells us that the Buddha did indeed have a senior disciple named Mahakashyapa, who seems to have actually succeeded the Buddha in leading his community in the wake of his death. His claimed successor in the Zen lineage, the Buddha's cousin and lifelong attendant, the Venerable Ananda, was also a real person, who played a central role with Mahakashyapa in convening the first Buddhist council that served to systematize the Buddha's teaching and legacy. However, beyond this, much of the Zen lineage stretching through twenty-eight generations to the Indian monk Bodhidharma is a creative construct that freely weaves facts with myths, and myths with dreams. That is until somewhere around the death of the famed sixth ancestor of the Zen school, Huineng, in 713 AD, when the Zen lineage begins to memorialize history, reflecting the movement of a then well-established and generally accepted, unique, spiritual school.

Prior to Huineng, Zen mythology asserts that the Buddha's robe and begging bowl were transmitted as physical proof of the succession to the spiritual mantel of the Buddha, from one master to one disciple in each generation. After Huineng, however, the institution of dharma transmission became standardized in such a way that multiple successors to the Buddha's lineage could co-exist at any given time. At first these successors were typically the heads of temples and monasteries, and dharma transmission was given from the abbot to their heir apparent (of the literal spiritual and legal headship of the temple and its property). Today, though, dharma transmission generally is offered to Zen followers who are thought to have come to embody the most profound realization of the Zen way, and who have become representatives of the lineage with teaching and training the next generation of Zen students.

Understanding that religion in general, including Buddhism, is a human enterprise, composed by humans and for humans, we can come to appreciate its sometimes-messy development, and its often-indirect navigation of socio-political forces as it seeks survival and relevance. Zen should not be given a free pass from criticism, either philosophical or historical, but it should also not be needlessly deconstructed by extreme forces of so-called rational inquiry that might render its mythology and poetry lifeless. There is truth that exists beyond history, and transformative power to be found in the stories we tell about how and why we have arrived at this very moment. Zen employs these tools alongside genuinely precise, generationally refined methods of meditation and inquiry to help guide its adherents to lives of meaning marked with suffering. Its teachers and students alike, even those profoundly realized, are always humans first and foremost, most extraordinary in their ordinariness, which is the very heart of awakening in the Zen vein.

EXPLORING YOUR PRESUPPOSITIONS

It has been noted in this chapter that Buddhism is a spiritual tradition that openly employs metaphors, analogies, and hagiography. For many, this may be a new way of thinking, outside of the typical presentation of grand stories as fact in other religious traditions. As you set out to explore the Zen tradition, it can be useful to explore your own beliefs and judgements that may color how you interpret the content in the chapters to come. In Buddhism it is said that it is best to empty your cup before trying to fill it back up. However, if we don't know that our cups are full, or what they are full of, it can be difficult to discern how much room to make, and where to appropriately pour out the contents to make that room.

Thoughtfully consider the following questions. Write your answers down and refer to them over the course of reading this text, paying attention to how your answers evolve.

1. What is the purpose of religion?

2. What is the nature of truth?

3. Can non-historical stories teach truth?

4. Does metaphor have a place in religious practice?

5. On what basis should one form beliefs?

6. What is the role of faith in religious practice?

7. Does a religion have to answer all of life's tough questions to be valuable and followed, or is there room for unknowing?

8. Do you have a lineage of people from your past who aren't related to you, but have influenced and supported you as a sort of spiritual family?

ZEN ART
AS A PRACTICE PATH

Zen art is not *only* an expression and extension of the awakened mind; it can also constitute a practice path. Studying authentic Zen art and walking in its footsteps through the practice of a given discipline in reference to awakened exemplars can also facilitate realization. In reality, this is a very advanced level of cultivation, and the neophyte practitioner would likely be better served by first establishing themselves well in the primary disciplines of the Zen way. But, while there are sincerely given and generally applicable guidelines to the Zen path, there are few absolute rules, and exceptions abound (hence, again, the centrality of the Zen teacher in directing the practice path, especially in its burgeoning stages). If one's heart is truly moved to study Zen at any stage, that is to say, if one finds a karmic affinity with it, there is no time like the present to set foot to the path of awakening.

When people talk about their own art, they often describe how they feel during the artistic process as "Zen." Consider the following questions. As you read the book, reflect back on your answers to see how they have changed as you learn.

1. Think about your own artistic process and how it makes you feel.

2. What do you feel after your project is complete? A sense of calm, or exhilaration?

3. How can you extend that feeling further into your daily life, creating more of a path than a singular project?

4. If you were to establish a routine where you regularly set aside time for art, how do you think your outlook might shift?

CHAPTER 2

ZEN'S KEY TEACHINGS

Having bounded from its birthplace in China and then grown deep roots in Korea, Japan, and Vietnam, the Zen tradition today has stretched around the globe. Zen schools, centers, temples, and teachers can now be found throughout the world, representing many diverse (and yet legitimate) sub-schools and lineages with much in common, but also with many distinctives uniquely developed over time. While the central task of awakening has remained firmly intact in all authentic Zen traditions, the methods employed to move students in its direction, alongside images and metaphors used toward that aim, have diversified significantly as the Zen wind has blown from continent to continent. Perhaps most interesting in the current evolution of the wider tradition is the emerging Zen lineages of the Western world, which have been profoundly marked by their encounter with the religions, languages, and cultures of Europe and the Americas over the past one hundred years or so.

ZEN AND BELIEF

Zen in the West has jettisoned the metaphysical literalism that has accompanied the tradition, particularly in its folk form, from the time of its emergence in the ancient Indus River Valley to the present. In some cases, the sweeping reforms of the tradition into late modernity and postmodernity by Western people have been problematically simplistic. In other cases, though, the recasting of ancient metaphors by contemporary people in the light of interdisciplinary observation has deepened the wider Zen tradition and influenced it in its native contexts. It would be impossible to talk about the key teachings of Zen without examining this phenomenon, particularly in a text specifically written with Western audiences in mind.

In 1997, former Buddhist monk and current Buddhist teacher Stephen Batchelor published a then-controversial work entitled *Buddhism Without Beliefs: A Contemporary Guide to Awakening.* In doing so, Batchelor gave voice to a quiet but sizeable number of Westerners who were sympathetic to many of the teachings of Buddhism, in which they found clear articulations of the human condition and accessible answers to the problem of suffering, but who were nonetheless at odds with the supernatural assumptions that accompanied those answers. Batchelor sought to question if and how one could seriously practice Buddhism while not adopting idiosyncratic beliefs in reincarnation, cosmic karmic abacuses, and retinues of invisible beings. The answer that Batchelor arrived at (alongside a great many Buddhist sympathizers and practitioners around the world, it turns out) was an unequivocal yes.

To some, particularly those afflicted with strong bouts of "all or nothing thinking," a living spiritual tradition that openly recognizes its own internal challenges to doctrine and ongoing evolution could seem problematic. After all, how could a tradition that has taken seriously various metaphysical concepts easily dissolved in the light of current scientific observation, have anything valuable or authoritative to say about the human condition? To put it simply, it can, and the proof is in the reality that it does shed a light on the human condition as experienced by millions of practitioners, and the advent of Buddhist-informed medical and psychological modalities such as mindfulness-based interventions to pain and stress.

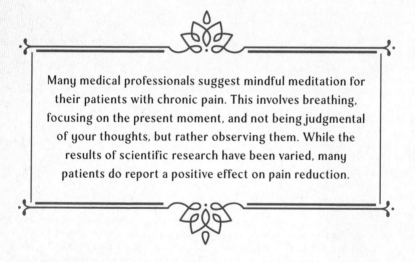

Many medical professionals suggest mindful meditation for their patients with chronic pain. This involves breathing, focusing on the present moment, and not being judgmental of your thoughts, but rather observing them. While the results of scientific research have been varied, many patients do report a positive effect on pain reduction.

AWAKENING

The present text, like Batchelor's skeptical tome, and indeed all Zen instruction of any weight, is ultimately a guide to awakening. But what is awakening outside of the likely errant metaphysical assumptions about reincarnation, grand karmic consequence, and multiple planes of existence? The exact nature of awakening, and its assumed baggage specifically, is somewhat debatable among various Zen schools. However, this is more a result of the limitations of language than it is a lack of sufficiently common experience that can be agreed upon as the realization deemed as awakening.

In short form, it might be understood that awakening is essentially a profound recalibration to reality, whereupon it becomes difficult to fall back out of accord with it. This recalibration essentially recasts one's understanding of the notion of selfhood, subject-object dualism, time, space, and the suffering matrix itself, while along the way honing perception through concentration, allaying existentialist angst with clear insight, and assuming the reins of meaning-making through stewardship of mind and body (thought and action). You may notice very little, if any, appeal in this definition to fantastical and otherworldly claims. The point is that the pinnacle cultivation of Zen practice is rooted in ordinary life, in ordinary human bodies, amidst ordinary human concerns. While there is nearly infinite poetry and flourish that could be added to this description, there is little need to embellish the reality of awakening to make it any more titillating or challenging. If you find the notion of awakening (also known as enlightenment) somewhat vast and even foreign, you're likely in the right place.

ZEN PHILOSOPHY

Zen practice is inextricably linked to Zen philosophy. Meditation without a supportive framework to define its purpose and direct its progression differs little from daydreaming or sleeping. While many Zen resources seek to throw would-be practitioners into the essential practices of the tradition as soon as possible (noting the common pitfall of spending too much time ruminating about reality and meditation, and not enough on accessing reality through meditation), the present writer finds it essential to establish parameters, some broad and some exacting, for beginning such practice responsibly.

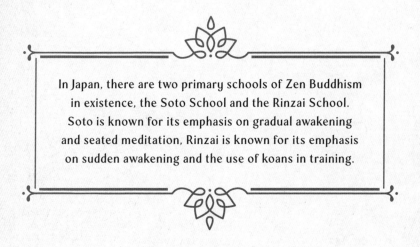

In Japan, there are two primary schools of Zen Buddhism in existence, the Soto School and the Rinzai School. Soto is known for its emphasis on gradual awakening and seated meditation, Rinzai is known for its emphasis on sudden awakening and the use of koans in training.

Different teachers and different lineages rely upon varied concepts and resources to direct students in the practice of Zen, and while there are many common principles and texts, few lineages, teachers, or centers (especially in the West) employ standardized courses of study. In keeping with the postmodern, global perspective of the present text, we will examine seven key teachings of the Zen tradition, to establish a toolkit of essential philosophical resources that will inform any subsequent practice(s), namely *no self*, part and parcel of One Reality, experienced through Two Perspectives, and marked with Three Seals, which are integrated into the Four Noble Truths, practiced with Five Precepts, and manifest as Six Perfections. Let's break that down.

NO SELF

It is hardly debated that the most fundamental teaching of Buddhism and Zen is that of non-self (or *anitya*, in Sanskrit). As was noted in the opening chapter, non-self was the fundamental concept that decisively birthed the Buddhist tradition as a distinct spiritual movement from the prevailing proto-Hindu religious milieu of the Buddha's time and place. Frankly speaking, most every form of human suffering can be traced back to an errant sense of substantial selfhood, that through decades of misoriented perception comes to be viewed and imagined as real. The assumed self is the lynchpin upon which innumerable forms of suffering hinge and take root, and yet when closely investigated, it is nowhere to be found!

When asked about the nature of the self, most people immediately begin appealing to various adjectives that they most commonly identify with as individuals. When confronted with the reality that these descriptors are most always referencing attributes rather than the objective self, appeals will then be made to the body itself. Noting the linguistic quandary posed by inferring a possessor as non-distinct from possession (i.e. "*my* body," etc.), the most common response is confused silence, which may serve as a gateway to proper meditation.

Human beings spend a lot of time propping up their sense of self while fearing and trying to stave off its inevitable demise, battling a predetermined skirmish with what more than one teacher has defined as the primal wound (that is, an inability to reconcile with impermanence when situated amidst an assumption of a concrete sense of self). The invitation and assertion of Zen around the notion of non-self is to realize that the very notion of an independent and stable sense of self is the catalyst for human suffering (as distinct from pain), and that in letting go of errant views of the self and coming into awareness, acceptance, and accord with the reality of non-self, the problems (that is, suffering) can dissolve along with it.

ONE REALITY

Zen Buddhism asserts that reality is a process rather than a product. This process is not different from reality itself, which in classical Sanskrit terminology is called *sunyata*. Sunyata has been variously described in English vernacular as "a ground of being" and a primordial void; as the experience underpinning notions of God, as the quantum field itself, and as the very creative potency that gives rise to form, and which receives and recycles it upon its dissolution—zero-ness.

In essence, reality is unstable and impermanent and all potentials existing and non-existing relate in constant dynamic tension and flux. Sunyata may best be understood as the notion that all things are devoid of a stable, concrete existence. When anything is examined closely, it breaks apart into infinite arrays of constituent parts. These parts too are generally comprised of smaller parts often shared with other things, all the way to the subatomic level (and seemingly beyond). Think of an atom, then zoom out and see molecules, zoom out further and see wood, further still, a table leg, then yet even further, a table. Here, logic tends to reach its limits, and waves and particles merge freely into one another. Seeming quandaries—such as where the table begins and where it ends—become conceptually feasible, too, and ultimately disruptive of our common casting of reality as a realm of the manifest and distinct.

Zen practice may be understood to be essentially concerned with the direct perception of non-self and sunyata (the One Reality). It is from the experience and integration of the nature of being that all realization and wisdom on the Zen path bounds. The primary formula for overcoming suffering is to cast away the unreal assumptions of reality and being, and to become aware of, accept, and come into continual harmony with the nature of reality as it is, and as we are.

TWO PERSPECTIVES

The Two Perspectives on reality (sunyata) is a teaching that is certainly complex. Also known as the "Two Truths doctrine," this teaching postulates that the *experience* of reality differs from the actual *nature* of reality. The world of common experience is known as the realm of the relative, whereas the intentional encounter with the nature of reality is known as the realm of the absolute. The absolute and relative perspectives co-exist in harmony and dynamic tension in the awakened mind, but they are often irreconcilable to cognition rooted in the mutually exclusive, branched thinking of the un-awakened mind.

To put the realm of relative perception and experience into perspective, one may look toward any object. Let's go back to the table mentioned earlier. Clearly, the table is a table. It is made of wood, with a flat surface secured to four or more legs. It is stable enough to support things placed atop it and barring no unforeseen disasters it will persist as a table, identifiable as such even to strangers who have never encountered it before, in both form and function, for the foreseeable future. This is the realm of the relative.

In reality there is no such thing as a table, and table-ness is not a distinct ontology. If one were to remove the table's legs, where does its table-nature go? At what point does a table assume its table nature as a gestalt—that is, something that is more than the sum of its parts? At what point does it devolve back into merely its constituent parts (table legs, a tabletop, and perhaps pins, bolts, screws, and glue)? If the table is set ablaze and is reduced to ash, where did its table-ness go? This is the absolute view, namely that the table is never really a table, and its constituent parts are never really those things either. Wood, one major element of the table, is a fibrous, treated material, which is a combination of organic matter nurtured into being by sunlight, water, earth, and time, which at the molecular level is comprised of ever smaller and smaller particles. In the truest sense, there is nothing to be called a table, or wood for that matter. These terms are just labels that serve to relate to a perceived object. To regard them as anything else is to give rise to poor understanding when reality shows (time and time again) its folly, most clearly when things come undone. Things, like people, possess no self-nature. Individuality and permanence are ultimately relative distinctions, illusions that, while sometimes functional, serve to divide the singular fabric of reality and its interdependent nature into unreal constructs.

In the course of human life it is impossible to abide peacefully in either the relative or absolute perspective exclusively. Rather, one must come to understand the outer and inner nature of all phenomena, and perceive their ultimately indistinct, inter-dwelling states of being in real time. To become truly aware of this type of integrated perception is generally a long-term process, which comprises advanced Zen practice after a thorough, experiential introduction to sunyata has occurred.

THE THREE SEALS

At this point, the content of the Three Seals teaching has been thoroughly introduced, and the concept itself is perhaps best understood as a convenient carrying case for a unified description of reality. The Three Seals are impermanence (anitya, in Sanskrit), insubstantiality (aka non-self, or *anatman* in Sanskrit), and unsatisfactory-ness (dukkha). It should be noted that in some portions of Buddhist scripture, the third seal of unsatisfactory-ness is sometimes taught as nirvana (the extinguishing of dukkha). Ultimately this distinction is of little importance, as dukkha and nirvana are only superficially oppositional and really reflect two sides, or Two Perspectives, of one coin.

The Three Seals teaching serves to remind us that all experiences and phenomena that we could possibly encounter are, at their core: temporal, unstable, and passing; comprised of endless constituent and shared parts and therefore possess no self-nature; and prone to give rise to suffering and dissatisfaction when regarded in any other way.

THE FOUR
NOBLE TRUTHS

While the Four Noble Truths have already been thoroughly discussed in chapter one, as part of this book's effort to situate the Zen school within the wider Buddhist tradition, their importance to the Zen project cannot be stressed enough. To phrase the Four Noble Truths in a slightly more accessible way, it might be understood that un-awakened life is tinged by suffering and dissatisfaction (dukkha) because human beings are prone to experiencing life and things in ways that belie their true nature, and when their true or actual nature is revealed our cognitive dissonance gives rise to frustration and lamentation (samudaya); there is a way to bring dissatisfaction and suffering to an end, in this very life (nirodha); the way to manifest this end is to awaken to seeing things as they are, rather than as they are not, and act in accord with that vision (marga).

The Four Noble Truths essentially formulate a roadmap to awakening and serve to maintain the focus and relevance of one's practice efforts. If a teaching or technique cannot be easily mapped onto the structural schema of the Four Noble Truths, it is likely that the teaching or technique is working toward objectives other than awakening, and one's motivation and direction in employing it likely needs to be re-examined. The mind is exceptionally skilled at leading practitioners down roads that do not threaten its own relative integrity, and as such the mind is primed to accept and even pursue a great many suppositions and methods alike that could distract practitioners from experiencing the reality of their own temporal and insubstantial nature. It is therefore exceedingly important to keep the root teaching of the Four Noble Truths at the center of one's practice.

> The Four Noble Truths are the primary teaching
> upon which all of the world's Buddhists can agree.
> While there may be disagreements about how
> to cultivate the specific aims of the Buddhist path,
> the Four Noble Truths are universally recognized for their
> exceptionally accurate portrayal of the human condition.

THE FIVE PRECEPTS

The practice of the precepts will be explored in much more depth in chapter three, but in seeking to enshrine their place as a core teaching and practice in the Zen tradition, it must be said that precepts are a primary way that practitioners can traverse the path (marga) toward the cessation of suffering (nirodha). While cultivating awakening is at the heart of the Zen project, unless vision is integrated into one's actions, life awakening cannot be manifest. In this, precepts are both a starting and finishing point in cultivating awakening, both in vision and action.

The Five Precepts invite us to examine our regard for five domains of human behavior, namely life, possession, sexuality, truth, and sobriety. Typically framed as five instructions to not kill, steal, engage in sexual misconduct, lie, or become intoxicated, the precepts are less rules than they are invitations to awareness in where and how these actions could take place. Precepts practice is self-regulated, as is nearly all spiritual practice, and breaking even the spirit of the precepts is typically regarded as inevitable rather than supremely avoidable. It might be understood then that precepts are much more logical than regulatory in nature.

Various Buddhist movements have gradually adopted many more possible precepts than these five, but all hold these five in common, and prescribe them to both lay and ordained practitioners alike. Precepts are thought to embody integrated awakened action. Engaging the practice of precepts fully demands that the practitioner attend mindfully to the whole of their life, which in turn cultivates wisdom through awakened vision, which then manifests as awakened action (living out the precepts).

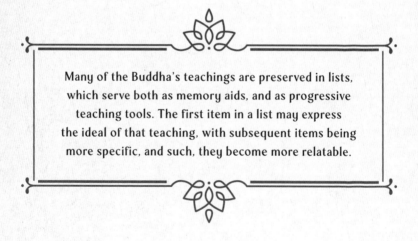

Many of the Buddha's teachings are preserved in lists, which serve both as memory aids, and as progressive teaching tools. The first item in a list may express the ideal of that teaching, with subsequent items being more specific, and such, they become more relatable.

THE SIX PERFECTIONS

The final key teaching to be traversed in this text is that of the Six Perfections. Given in Buddhist scripture as the perfection (*paramita*) of generosity (*dana*), virtue (*sila*), equanimity (*ksanti*), diligence (*virya*), concentration (*dhyana*), and wisdom (*prajna*), it may be understood that the Six Perfections are something akin to the "fruitages of the spirit" in Christianity, which for the Zen Buddhist are indicative of a mature practice. While these perfections may be pursued individually, the Zen tradition is more concerned with their spontaneous manifestation as a practitioner's life comes into deeper and deeper accord with their practice, and the vision of awakening. In this, the Six Perfections are more mile markers than individual pursuits or goals.

🌸 The perfection of generosity manifests as the reality of one's interdependence with all beings and dawns as an authentic experience combined with a thorough acceptance of the idea of the temporary, and a proper orientation toward ownership and possession gleaned through the practice of the precepts.

🌸 The perfection of virtue is the result of awakened vision being lived out, as the Two Perspectives become more and more integrated as one's default mode of perception.

🌸 The perfection of equanimity is the product of profound awareness and acceptance of the Three Seals, and the impact of their pull upon all phenomena, and manifests according to this vision.

🪷 The perfection of diligence is a form of energy gleaned from tapping into the ultimately mysterious nature of being and reality and surrendering comfortably to the implications of the limits of conceptual thought—it is in no small way energy aroused by the curiosity that is leaning into unknowing.

🪷 The perfection of concentration is the accurate perception cultivated in the practice of meditation, both formal sitting meditation and embodied forms otherwise.

🪷 Finally, the perfection of wisdom is the difficult-to-define quality of awareness, combined with understanding, and informing action (and inaction) that is displayed as the primary byproduct of awakening—it is a transcendent knowing that embodies the unconscious competence of mastery in any pursuit.

The Six Perfections can be utilized as motivators in one's practice, to help propel one toward awakening, especially in times when one's practice is proving difficult or stagnant. While (again) caution must be taken to not enshrine the Six Perfections as individual pursuits unto themselves, they are good reflection aids for use in approximating one's honest progress on the path to awakening.

The Zen Buddhist path in its varied iterations is strewn with literally innumerable teachings, and not all traditions cast the same teachings as central or key to their particular pedagogical and training paradigms. However, the teachings presented in this chapter would likely be accepted by most all Zen lineages as important and certainly nearly central to the project of awakening. As you progress into the practice of Zen, more and more teachings will become available to you, and it is important to not confuse the accumulation of knowledge with the cultivation of awakening. As the old Zen adage goes, all teachings are simply fingers pointing at the moon—if you never turn your head and align your gaze directly to the moon, the fingers and their pointing are of no use.

THE SIX PARAMITAS (PERFECTIONS)

布施　THE PERFECTION OF GENEROSITY

持戒　THE PERFECTION OF VIRTUE

忍辱　THE PERFECTION OF EQUANIMITY

精进　THE PERFECTION OF DILIGENCE

禅定　THE PERFECTION OF CONCENTRATION

般若　THE PERFECTION OF WISDOM

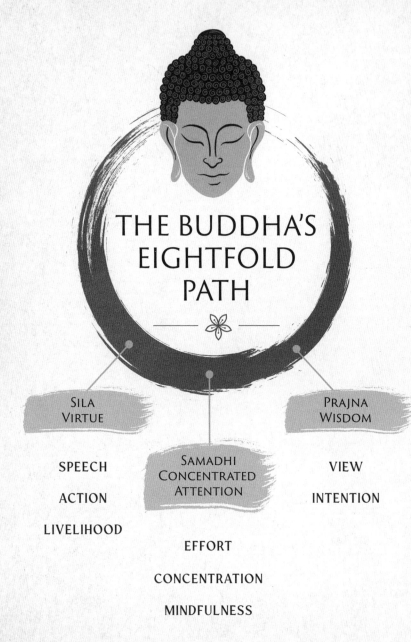

THE BUDDHA'S EIGHTFOLD PATH

SILA
VIRTUE

PRAJNA
WISDOM

SPEECH

SAMADHI
CONCENTRATED
ATTENTION

VIEW

ACTION

INTENTION

LIVELIHOOD

EFFORT

CONCENTRATION

MINDFULNESS

EVALUATING BELIEF SYSTEMS

The earlier exercise, Exploring Your Presuppositions, asked you to begin examining some of the presuppositions that you are arriving at with your survey of Zen Buddhism. From this, it's clear that we all arrive at most pursuits with substantial baggage in tow. When it comes to spirituality, we tend to have lots of beliefs that are derived from our life experiences, or even instilled in us from the spiritual practices of our upbringing.

For this exercise, reflect on the core teaching themes of this chapter, the possibility of awakening, of One Reality explored as Two Truths, marked with Three Seals, viewed through Four Noble Truths, practiced with Five Precepts, toward Six Perfections. Consider the following questions and write down your answers. Review them as you read through this book, and see how your perspectives are shifting.

1. Can humans find a way out of suffering in this lifetime? Does it seem that a mere shift in perspective makes that possible, or does something more cosmic need to come into play?

2. Zen's "Two Truths" posit an interplay between the polarities of our experience, rather than a binary reality locked in a battle of good versus evil. Can a good situation be a bad situation, and a bad situation be a good situation? Does position and perspective have the power to alter these categories?

3. While humans tend to universally long for stability and endurance, Zen teaches that all things are marked with impermanence, substantiality, and the seeds of both awakening and suffering alike. What things do you struggle to accept as impermanent and not comprised of any enduring self-nature?

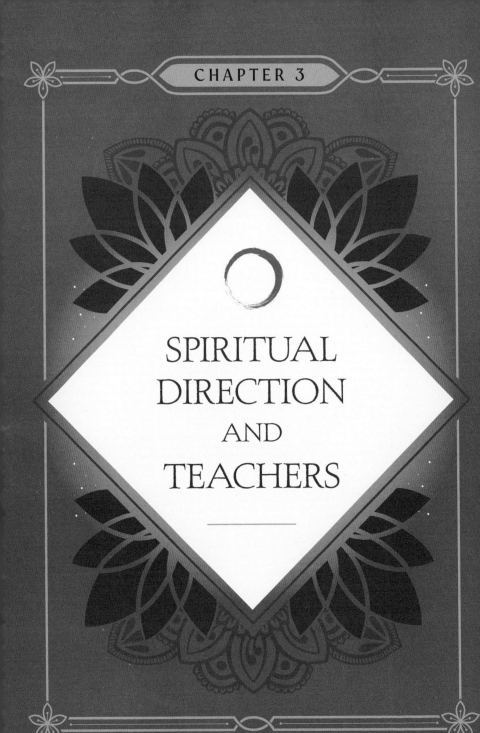

CHAPTER 3

SPIRITUAL
DIRECTION
AND
TEACHERS

To practice Zen in any traditional sense is to establish a relationship with a competent and qualified teacher at some point. Zen is not a self-directed activity, despite how much of the practice may actually be done alone or done alone-together (as in practicing meditation in a group). As has been noted elsewhere in this text, Zen is a living tradition, and its practice has been transmitted from teacher to student in verifiable succession for over a thousand years. It's not that one cannot explore Zen philosophy or experiment with Zen practice on their own, and even reap immense rewards from doing so, but it is true that to formally practice Zen one must work with a teacher.

Any text on Zen that denies or neglects the central teacher–student relationship would be incomplete and reflect a truly idiosyncratic form of Zen that stands outside of the entire history of the tradition. While subsequent chapters will spend considerable amounts of time detailing the types of practices that can be easily picked up and navigated well enough for the purposes of personal exploration without a teacher, they must be prefaced by a discussion of the nature of the Zen teaching relationship, its scope, and function. Seeing as the teacher ideally represents an awakened guide, capable of showing the way for others, the notion of Zen teachers must be examined in the context of awakening itself.

TYPES OF AWAKENING

Nearly from its inception, the wider Buddhist tradition has identified three primary types of awakened beings, namely Samyaksambuddhas, Pratyekabuddhas, and Arhats, with a later distinction being formulated placing Bodhisattvas on par with Arhats.

SAMYAKSAMBUDDHAS

Samyaksambuddhas are awakened beings that are liberated and enlightened by means of their own efforts, who achieve such profound insight that they are essentially able to establish new practice paths capable of leading other beings to awakening. This type of awakening is understood to be exceptionally rare in history, and is often only attributed to the Shakyamuni Buddha, Siddhartha Gautama.

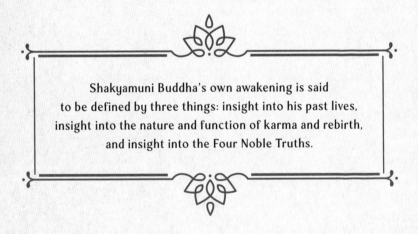

Shakyamuni Buddha's own awakening is said
to be defined by three things: insight into his past lives,
insight into the nature and function of karma and rebirth,
and insight into the Four Noble Truths.

PRATYEKABUDDHAS

Pratyekabuddhas are beings who, like Samyaksambuddhas, are awakened by means of their own efforts, without the aid of teachers or guides, but whose quality of realization either renders them disinterested or incapable of leading others to awakening. Like Samyaksambuddhas, Pratyekabuddhas are generally considered an exceptional rarity.

ARHATS

Arhats are beings who come to complete awakening by following the dispensation of a Samyaksambuddha and are capable of instructing others in those methods and modes so that they too may arrive at the so-called *other shore* of awakening. While all awakening may be understood to be relatively uncommon among the general populace, the awakening of an Arhat is considered completely attainable with the clear-eyed guidance of a similarly realized teacher.

BODHISATTVAS

Bodhisattvas are essentially beings awakened in the same manner as Arhats, but whose primary motivation for awakening is not personal liberation, but the collective liberation of *all* sentient beings. It is the opinion of the present author that the Bodhisattva ideal is more a matter of pedagogy than ontology, wherein the interdependence known to the awakened is co-opted as a form of skillful means (*upaya* in Sanskrit) to ignite a sense of zeal and energetic drive to arrive at awakening in not-yet-realized students of the way. No doubt certain people do not possess (in reference to their own individual suffering) sufficient motivation to traverse the path of awakening, but in pursuit of collective benefit for all sentient beings they may find the vigor to pursue awakening in full.

THE FUNCTION OF TEACHERS

In understanding the types of awakened beings known to the Zen Buddhist tradition over time, we can begin to understand the importance of having a realized teacher who can guide one along the path of awakening. That said, Zen masters ought not be confused with gurus, as otherwise known to the world of popularized Eastern religions. Zen teachers are exemplars—that is, practitioners first and teachers as needed. A Zen teacher's primary tool is their personal example, which alone can help guide the keen-eyed student in the particulars of awakening. Zen teachers are wise guides who can point the way and verify one's place along the way; their authority is gleaned not solely from some esoteric installation into a religious hierarchy, but rather through their personal gravity and insight. Whereas the guru must be surrendered to, the Zen master's tutelage finds acceptance through their ability to demonstrate its results and to defend its integrity in the free exchange of critique and question known as "dharma combat" or "Zen dialogue."

Practically speaking, the primary responsibilities of a Zen teacher include initiating students into the Zen way through officiating precept and refuge ceremonies (*jukai* in Japanese), leading regular meditation practice, and intensive extended retreats (*zazenkai*, *sesshin*, and *ango* in Japanese, depending on the length), alongside meeting students in private sessions (known variously as *dokusan* and *sanzen* in Japanese) where students may ask questions, present the insights and fruits of their practice, and/or meet with the teacher for the examination of Zen case studies (*koankufu* in Japanese).

While some Zen teachers are also monks and priests, not all monks and priests are Zen teachers in the sense of being formally authorized lineage holders, empowered to take on personal students. Indeed, the practice of spiritual direction of Zen teachers is distinct from the public ministry of Zen priests and monks. While spiritual direction is an intensely personal, dedicated, and ongoing relationship between a Zen teacher and a Zen student, priestcraft is essentially concerned with the facilitation of public ceremonies and life celebrations common to the Buddhist liturgical calendar and appendant to various life transitions (such as baby naming and welcoming ceremonies, weddings, home and vehicle blessings, funerals, and the like). Ordained practice and its accompanying public ministry are unique forms of Zen training that are outside of the scope of the present work, but suffice it to say, from the very beginning of Buddhism there have always been monks and priests intrinsic to the tradition, and it is possible in many places to dedicate the whole of one's life formally to the pursuit of awakening through rites of monastic and priestly ordination. This dedication, though, does not necessarily make one a Zen teacher or authorize the ordained practitioner to offer any form of spiritual direction.

FINDING A TEACHER

Different lineages of Zen offer various empowerments and authorizations along the way to becoming a fully-fledged Zen teacher, and when setting out to find a competent spiritual director in the Zen tradition it is important to find a teacher with the appropriate credentials (generally dharma transmission, known variously in Japanese as *denbo*, *shiho*, or *inka shomei*), received from a reputable teacher within a generally recognized lineage. There is no such thing as a legitimate Zen teacher that stands outside of a lineage succession. That said, lineage itself (as has been discussed earlier in this text) is not always a crystal-clear matter. Even among generally recognized lines, the qualities of genuinely authorized teachers can vary significantly, so it is important to find a teacher with whom you can establish a sense of trust.

It is not the job of Zen teachers to be infinitely agreeable or accessible. Zen is not an evangelical spiritual tradition, and it does not entail any traditions of religious proselytization. In fact, the opposite is quite true. Especially in times past, but certainly today in more traditional practice settings, it was common for seekers to be turned away from monasteries and temples at least several times, before finally and somewhat begrudgingly being allowed to enter and train. Following this, a number of months or even years of seemingly ancillary and even unrelated work might ensue before the trainee would be viewed as a serious student of the way, properly committed to the practice to finally begin receiving instruction in its innermost methods of psycho-spiritual formation. There is a wisdom saying, often employed by Western-born Zen teachers, that notes when it comes to the spiritual path it's best to not get started, but once started it's best to finish. This aphorism encapsulates the traditional rigor associated with setting serious foot to the ways of this tradition.

Zen training is ultimately a physically, psychologically, and spiritually demanding endeavor. It is not always comfortable or easy. The physical processes of Zen practice, such as sitting for extended amounts of time in silent meditation, can cause the body to ache and the knees to creak; the suppositions of Zen philosophy can disrupt our sense of equilibrium as they challenge the fundamental assumptions about reality that we've developed, as well as the methods in which we've learned to cope with it too. Zen training is ultimately a religious endeavor, and its themes can evoke conflict with religious experiences, commitments, and traumas that we've otherwise held.

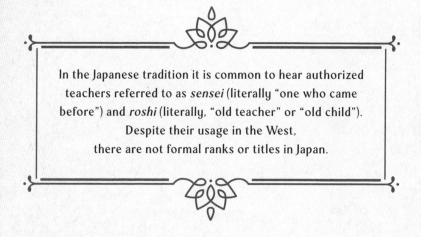

In the Japanese tradition it is common to hear authorized teachers referred to as *sensei* (literally "one who came before") and *roshi* (literally, "old teacher" or "old child"). Despite their usage in the West, there are not formal ranks or titles in Japan.

It should be understood that one must find a qualified Zen teacher in whom they can put their trust to support and guide them, foremost through the integrity of their own practice, but also with their ability to articulate their insights gleaned in specific and relatable ways.

The karmic body of a teacher and that of an aspiring student may not always mesh harmoniously, therefore it is important to practice discernment when committing to a teacher, and you can rest assured that the teacher will be involved in the same when deciding to commit to a potential student. One must not accept the tutelage of the first qualified teacher that they encounter simply because of convenience or proximity to one's locale.

In the contemporary era there are a number of avenues of practice accessible to students that would be inconceivable to previous generations of students. While Zen centers and temples themselves are relatively spread out in the Western World, typically clustered in large cities (with a more rural offering occasionally making an appearance), modern telecommunication methods have enabled qualified teachers to engage students in real time and across great distances. In this, students may connect with qualified spiritual directors in the Zen vein with whom they share a karmic affinity, rather than simply accepting what is locally available.

Many properly transmitted Zen teachers offer forms of online and hybrid training that have made Zen more accessible now than in any other time in history. With retreats (*zazenkai* and *sesshin*), private meetings with teachers (dokusan and sanzen), and even Zen case study practice (koankufu) now being offered online, Zen students can build a consistent practice, amidst an established community, and with a quality teacher than can easily be augmented through various in-person practice opportunities.

One may wonder what is meant by the phrase "karmic connection" offered here in relation to the mutual meeting and committing of potential students and teachers. Generally, it is understood that in a proper Zen Buddhist context, the likely familiar term of *karma* is a short form of the longer Sanskrit phrase karma-vipaka, which essentially references the ultimately mysterious mixture of conditions, experiences, causes, and effects that can come to harmoniously mesh into something productive. There are no hard-and-fast rules that can determine whether a student–teacher relationship will work or not. In this, one must look toward the facts of the teacher's qualifications and history, in addition to their personal qualities, and one's access to them. It is important to not put too much or too little stock into matters of reputation (in a world where online opinions and information comprise a nearly infinite array of facts). In short, a potential student of the Zen way should discern and trust their gut, be ready to be challenged but also affirmed in noting the general qualities and experiences that they are seeking, and not make hasty commitments to any community or teacher (and be wary of communities and teachers who are quick to do the same on their own end).

WORKING WITH A TEACHER

Once connected to a community and teacher with whom one student has found the seeds of karmic affinity and potential, the next steps may seem a little unclear. Suffice it to say that while continually showing up to practice is what constitutes practice, the Zen tradition is full of ritualistic and ceremonial matters relating to endeavors, commitments, and experiences. When it comes to establishing a formal relationship with a teacher, there is often a specific rite (frequently known as *shoken*) that will often accompany the commitment. While some communities have very clear processes and codified manners for approaching these rites, others do not. At the heart of the various possible traditions and rites, though, is the act of posing the question. Since antiquity, Buddhist teachers and clerics have been committed to only offering instruction to those expressly asking for it.

In many Japanese-descending Zen schools, requesting the formal tutelage of a teacher is as simple as approaching them in a private audience (dokusan) and offering three bows, posing the question, and gifting the teacher-to-be with a box of incense (a traditional gift formally symbolizing the request). The act of petitioning the teacher, though, is not merely symbolic in most cases, and the teacher's own assessment of the blossoming connection between them must be allowed adequate space in the equation for any true relationship to take legitimate root.

That said, generally by the time it has become appropriate for the student to pose the formal question of becoming a teacher's student, they likely already know the outcome of the inquiry.

In some schools, the formal relationship with a teacher is solidified through the rite of jukai, or receiving the Buddhist lay precepts. During jukai (which will be discussed in some depth in the next chapter) a student makes a number of commitments and receives a number of training guidelines (which are the precepts themselves), and further are often given a Buddhist name to use within the context of Zen training (a remnant of the expressly monastic origins of all schools of Buddhism). In such cases, similar to the rite of shoken, receiving the precepts, or jukai, must be expressly requested by the student at an appropriate time.

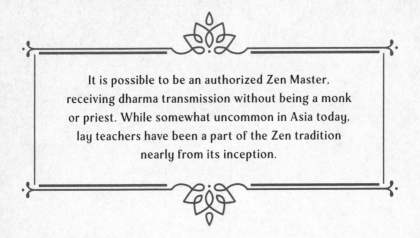

It is possible to be an authorized Zen Master, receiving dharma transmission without being a monk or priest. While somewhat uncommon in Asia today, lay teachers have been a part of the Zen tradition nearly from its inception.

Once a relationship with a qualified Zen teacher has been established, questions may arise as to the particular nature of the relationship, and what it looks like in function, throughout the course of a Zen student's practicing life. While the high-level functions of a teacher have been fleshed out earlier in this chapter, it should be reiterated that the central and primary commitment of a teacher is to function as a catalyst for awakening in the student. Zen has no other aim but the realization and manifestation of awakened living. And while for the lay student in particular, the Zen teacher's role is not to be expressly directive in matters outside of the processes of actual Zen practice, it can sometimes be difficult to define the bounds of such practice. That said, properly qualified Zen teachers will rarely prescribe behaviors or attitudes but rather will tend to engage in the characteristic dialogue of the Zen tradition that may be constructive, deconstructive, or genuinely inquisitive in nature, and thereby point the student toward awakened perception so that they may organically manifest wise action.

Different teachers and communities will offer diverse forms and modes of connecting with the community and teacher alike. The most common manners of working with a Zen teacher entail receiving their teaching at public practice opportunities such as weekly services and retreats (where public addresses, sometimes called *teisho* are frequently offered), in regularly scheduled private meetings (dokusan) that often are included in retreat schedules and even monthly Zen center calendars, and increasingly, in regularly scheduled individual instruction times (which may even take place on the internet), commonly known as *daisan*. It is of utmost importance that serious Zen students hoping to approach awakening make as many regular points of contact as may be possible with their teacher, practice community, and personal meditative disciplines. The more contact one maintains with their practice, the greater the likelihood of catching a glimpse of awakening, and thereby transforming one's suffering into the nirvanic abiding that practice aims to evoke.

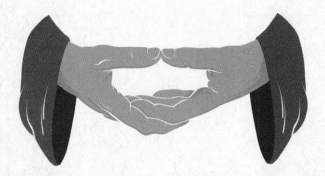

EXPLORING ONE'S RELATIONSHIP WITH SPIRITUAL LEADERS

Reflect on your relationships to spiritual teachers, figureheads, and clergy in your life. The centrality of the student-teacher relationship to formal Zen practice is undeniable and yet the reality is that many people coming to Zen do so as converts from other traditions where they may have had both good and poor interactions with clergy. Think about how these experiences and positions may help or hinder you on the Zen path. Remember, healthy skepticism is most welcome.

🌿 What questions would it be important for you to have answered before deciding to explore spiritual life in a Zen community?

🌿 What would you hope to gain by potentially working with a teacher?

🌿 Where do you imagine hang-ups would occur?

🌿 In what arenas or ways do you imagine that such a relationship could prove easy and even enlightening?

CHAPTER 4

LIFE BY VOW AND PRECEPTS

Like the spiritual direction of the student and teacher relationship, life by vow—that is, the practice of precepts—has been a part of the Buddhist path since its very beginning. Precepts are typically bestowed by qualified Zen lineage holders, or even in the witness of several of them (depending on the specific Zen school), and they comprise a foundational manner of Zen practice. Indeed, the professing of precepts typically forms the foundation for establishing oneself as a formal disciple of the Zen way.

Precepts are situated within an arena of Buddhist practice known as the Threefold Training (*trisiksa* in Sanskrit), which instructs that training in virtue (*sila*), chiefly by way of the moral considerations and ethical conduct elicited in precepts practice, gives way to concentrated attention (*samadhi*), which in turn yields the wisdom of awakened vision (*prajna*) through the practice of awareness, acceptance, and accord, of and with reality as it is. This awakened wisdom, or *prajna*, is the very root from which virtue grows as a harmonious response to the awareness and acceptance of reality. Thus, sila becomes samadhi, which yields prajna, and ultimately, again manifests sila. Therefore, it may be understood that precepts practice is both at the beginning and end of the wisdom cycle and is a practice well suited to both the deluded and the awakened alike. Indeed, the practice of precepts is in many ways indistinguishable from the living of an awakened life, though it can take many years of working with the precepts to near an understanding of the nuances of just how this is so.

THE CORRELATIONSHIP
OF THE THREE TRAINING (TRISIKSA)
AND THE SUBLIME TRAINING IN BUDDHISM

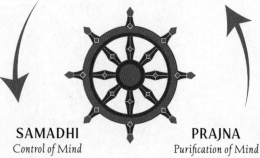

SILA
Morality

❧ No Killing ❧ No Stealing
No Sexual Misconduct ❧ No Lies ❧ No Intoxication

SAMADHI
Control of Mind

❧ Mindfulness
❧ Meditation

PRAJNA
Purification of Mind

❧ Wisdom

RECEIVING THE PRECEPTS

The formal taking of the Zen Buddhist precepts in the rite of jukai is often the first real step on the path of formalized Zen practice. In most centers, participating in jukai is predicated upon gaining basic familiarity with the fundamental practices common to a given community and its specific Zen lineage, and finding an affinity with those practices, then participating for some time in the life of the community so that mutual discernment may take place between the individual, the community, and the teacher regarding the appropriateness of a deepened mutual commitment.

During jukai, newly minted Zen students are usually invested with a token bib-like vestment (or *rakusu*) signifying the larger robes that monks and priests have received as primary clothing upon their ordination since the time of the Buddha. Alongside the rakusu, a dharma name (or *homyo*) is often bestowed upon the student, which is meant to inspire them to manifest the qualities described by the name in their practice. Traditionally monks and priests upon ordination would actually adopt the dharma name as their primary identity, as a form of renunciation, but for lay people in the modern world, there are many ways to relate to one's dharma name, and this can change over time. In some Zen lineages, it is common for the jukai participant to sew their own rakusu in the weeks leading up to the ceremony. While the rakusu and the homyo (usually inscribed on its reverse side) are perhaps the most tangible and visible signs of jukai, they are ultimately but a representation of a significant commitment to introspection and awakened activity.

In most Japanese descended Zen lineages, the commitments of jukai are threefold, involving taking refuge in the Triple Jewel, and professing two sets of precepts—the Three Pure Precepts, and the Ten Grave Precepts. This is unique, as in most Buddhist lineages it is common for lay practitioners to take refuge in the Triple Jewel, and to profess only the first five of the Ten Grave Precepts. Anything beyond this would typically constitute entrance into the monastic or priestly community. For a number of unique philosophical and socio-political reasons (too vast to describe here), in Japan, the sixteen commitments of jukai are the same for both lay and ordained practitioners, with ordained practitioners simply committing to a more specific container to exercise those commitments within, in a rite then known as *shukke tokudo*—literally the "leaving home" and entering the priestly order.

The word jukai is composed of *ju*, meaning to receive, while *kai* refers to the precepts, the literal translation meaning, "to receive the precepts." In this ceremony, the lay Zen Buddhist practitioner is officially welcomed to the path and receives precepts, marked by a public ceremony. It is during this time that the student receives their dharma name, a Zen name that helps to fold identity into practice.

The common commitment to life by vow, among both lay and ordained students alike, is a somewhat unique feature of Zen Buddhism that continues to emphasize that awakening is the sole objective of Zen practice. In the older Buddhist perspective, awakening was the business of monastics primarily, with lay people endeavoring to lead pious lives and to support the priestly community in their endeavor. Zen has no such distinction. To practice Zen is to strive for awakening, anything less cannot rightfully be termed Zen, especially in the view of most of the lineages that have successfully been transplanted and taken root in the global West.

PRACTICING WITH PRECEPTS

Because the specific nature of jukai common to many Zen traditions involves three sets of commitments, it will be helpful to examine the practice of Zen Buddhist precepts with a discussion of each of the separate elements that comprise the commitments of jukai, namely the Threefold Refuge, the Three Pure Precepts, and the Ten Grave Precepts.

THE THREEFOLD REFUGE

In Buddhist history, becoming a follower of the Buddha developed in several distinct phases. In the first phase, a potential disciple would simply be received by the Buddha with the uttering of a single phrase: "Come monk," proceeded then by a literal renunciation of one's worldly wealth, status, and location as the seeker became an actual itinerant follower of the Buddha. Gradually, though, as the body of the Buddha's followers grew, a bit more form had to be added to the equation to ensure an understanding of the actual commitments intrinsic to taking up the mantle of studying and applying the Buddha's dispensation in a communal setting. In this era, and persisting to the present day, the formula that was developed for a person to formally become a Buddhist was to take refuge in what is commonly called the Three Jewels (or *triratna*) of Buddha, Dharma, and Sangha.

In their original context, the Three Jewels (also sometimes known as the Triple Gem) referred to the actual person of Shakyamuni Buddha, his teachings (Dharma), and the community of monastic followers (Sangha). Through some 2,500 years of development, though, the Three Jewels have taken on a more nuanced meaning. In this, and in the Zen vein, we might understand Buddha as our own intrinsic (if not yet unmanifest) awakened nature, as well as in the whole body of reality of which we are a part. A *Mahayana* Buddhist teaching known as the *Trikaya*, or Three Bodies Doctrine, postulates that the historical Buddha Siddhartha Gautama exists in the realm of history and fact (that is, the relative world—*nirmanakaya*), but then extends the body of the Buddha to include the realm of the infinite and absolute (*dharmakaya*), and that of imagination and aspiration (*sambhogakaya*). Buddha is thus understood also as a metaphor for reality.

THE TRIKAYA DOCTRINE

Nirmanakaya

Buddha
as Person

Died at age 80

*The Body of History
and Fact*

Sambhogakaya

Buddha
as Ideal

*Archetypal
Buddha*

*The Body of Imagination
and Aspiration*

Dharmakaya

Buddha
as Reality

*Experience of
Ulitmate Truth*

*The Body of the Infinite
and Absolute*

Dharma is a relatively complex word. While most commonly translated as "teaching" or "law," in reference to the actual teachings of Shakyamuni Buddha, it also carries connotative definitions of "mental quality," "external phenomenon," and even "duty." Therefore, while we are certainly to exert ourselves in the application of the teachings and philosophy of Zen, we may once again understand dharma as a descriptor of reality itself and our commitments to it.

Finally, Sangha literally references the community of followers of the Buddha Dharma. In its original context, this referred explicitly to the ordained priests and monastics as a community of wise guides to the way, and among them it referenced collegial commitment and shared endeavor. In modern Western contexts, Sangha frequently is applied to the entire body of fellow Buddhists from whom we can draw (and provide) inspiration and support for our common work in cultivating awakening. While this more egalitarian vision is relatively new to the Buddhist ethos, it is one that has proven to have taken efficacious root around the world.

An analogy that may be helpful to understand the more overt application of taking refuge in Buddha, Dharma, and Sangha would be to equate the spiritual journey to a road trip, wherein Buddha or awakening itself comprises the destination, Dharma functions as a road map, and Sangha constitutes companions for the journey who can aid in reading the map, and even in driving from time to time. A more subtle and esoteric understanding of the Threefold Refuge might be to take refuge in our lives, from our lives, with our lives; to abide in the innate perfection of reality, by way of reality, supported by nothing but reality. In all Buddhist schools, reciting the Threefold Refuge aloud three times before an empowered Buddhist representative (or in extreme circumstances, before an image of the Buddha, or even simply with the intention of becoming Buddha) is the very act by which one formally becomes a follower of the Buddha way—that is, a Buddhist. While this act can ultimately be completed in the vernacular language of the disciple-to-be, it is very frequently, in formal ceremonial settings, offered in Pali, which is a dialect of Sanskrit close to what Siddhartha Gautama would have spoken:

Buddham Saranam Gacchami
I take refuge in the Buddha—the Awakened One, Nondifferent
from My Own Intrinsic Nature

Dhammam Saranam Gacchami
I take refuge in the Dharma—
the Enlightened Teaching and Reality Itself

Sangham Saranam Gacchami
I take refuge in the Sangha—
the Supreme Spiritual Community

BUDDHA   DHARMA   SANGHA

THE THREE PURE PRECEPTS

The Three Pure Precepts enjoy a long history in the Buddhist tradition, being embedded in both early Buddhist sources (such as the Dhammapada) and later scriptures (such as the Brahmajala Sutra). They encapsulate the spirit in which a disciple of the Zen way should move about the world, refraining from ill-doing, cultivating what is good, and being of service to all, whatever their stage may be in toward awakening. The Three Pure Precepts are often worded as follows:

I vow to refrain from all evil.
I vow to do only good.
I vow to benefit all beings.

Translating concepts through many languages and their appendant cultures is a difficult task, and often it involves more explanation than typical word-for-word translative efforts can provide. In this, the word "evil" in the Three Pure Precepts likely needs some fleshing out. In a Buddhist context, evil may be understood as the result of the unrestrained actualization of what is often called the Three Poisons of greed, anger, and ignorance. In Zen Buddhism, evil is not a self-existing phenomenon, but rather a combination of conditions that result in unskillful behavior. Actions and dispositions taken as a result of greed, of anger, or ignorance alone often result in immense suffering for ourselves and others, actions resulting from greed, anger, and ignorance together may be termed evil. To refrain from all evil is to pursue the wisdom that illuminates ignorance, transforms anger, and satiates the endless craving of greed; in short, this is how we pursue good. Saturated with the wisdom that allays evil and manifests good, we then naturally understand our condition as fundamentally interdependent beings, who cannot live but for or even as themselves, and thus who must live for the benefit of all beings, which we (as individuals) are also included within the collective body.

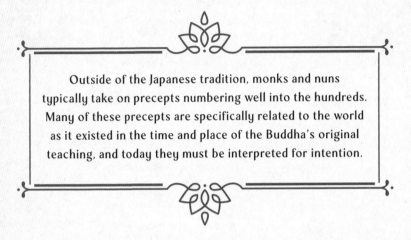

Outside of the Japanese tradition, monks and nuns typically take on precepts numbering well into the hundreds. Many of these precepts are specifically related to the world as it existed in the time and place of the Buddha's original teaching, and today they must be interpreted for intention.

In essence, the Three Pure Precepts are a vow to awaken. Having taken refuge in reality as it is, these precepts invite us to find in that refuge our true nature, which is already manifest and just waiting to be recognized. The Three Pure Precepts thus act as a mirror, holding reality on full display, allowing us to relatively toil in our practice until we realize the fundamental unity of where we are and where we think we are headed. Because this is somewhat abstract, the vows of jukai continue to add levels of actionability to our practice with the hope that successfully entering into the vision pointed toward by any one of these levels or precepts will help us enter into all of them at once.

THE TEN GRAVE PRECEPTS

The Ten Grave Precepts include the *pancasila* (the Five Precepts given to Buddhist students since the time of the Buddha). These are specific ethical and mindfulness teachings that direct us to harness the power of our minds to look deeply into our daily lives, not only to steer clear of actions that would arise from greed, anger, and ignorance (resulting then in the evil that harms ourselves and others alike), but also to remain checked into a dialogue with major themes such as the value of life, the limits of ownership, the power of sexuality, the nature of truth, and the importance of sobriety.

It should be noted here that in typical Western contexts, prone as they are to relying on familiar cultural themes that are often deeply influenced by Judeo–Christian thought, precepts are often equated to commandments, and they should not be. As discussed in chapter one, the Buddha was an occasional teacher, which means he taught in a way that reflected the assumptions and needs of a given audience in a specific context. The Buddha's teaching was not given once and for all time but rather was given with an intimate awareness of change as the only constant of life in the material world. In fact, for the monastic community, the body of precepts to be followed grew and grew with the community throughout the Buddha's life. It is recorded in the *Mahaparinirvana Sutra* that when the Buddha was nearing the end of his life, his disciples asked him not only who their teacher in his wake should be, but also which of the precepts laid out by him they should continue to follow. The Buddha responded by saying that his disciples should learn to be lamps unto themselves and that they should keep the major and discard the minor precepts, refusing to give further authoritative direction. The precepts and practices that endure today are those that bodies of Buddhist practitioners and adepts over time have gleaned to be exceptionally and enduringly useful in the pursuit of awakening, and they are tools to that effect, rather than laws to define worthiness or inclusion.

Precepts are elective guides toward a practice, likely among communities, that are not reflections of otherworldly hierarchies and realities, but which rather exist only here and now, when and where they in fact do exist. The only punishment to be doled out for the breaking of the precepts is that which may emanate according to the principles of karma-vipaka, conditional causation, and effect that they initiate or intersect with. The point of precept practice is not so much moral compliance with the edicts of a supernatural being, but the cultivation of intimate awareness in life's arenas of consequence.

While there are sincerely given and generally applicable guidelines to the Zen path, there are few absolute rules, and exceptions abound (hence, again, the centrality of the Zen teacher in directing the practice path, especially in its burgeoning stages). If one's heart is truly moved to study Zen at any stage, that is to say, if one finds a karmic affinity with it, there is no time like the present to set foot to the path of awakening.

The first Five Precepts are frequently translated as:

- ❧ I vow not to kill.
- ❧ I vow not to take what is not given.
- ❧ I vow not to misuse sexuality.
- ❧ I vow to refrain from false speech.
- ❧ I vow to refrain from intoxicants.

Rather humorously, it may be pointed out that in the most legalistic way these precepts in the original language and context forbid the killing of awakening beings (namely Buddhas) specifically, stealing of things worth more than "four rice grains' weight in gold" (something like one-twenty-fourth of a Troy ounce—about $75 at the time of this writing), specifically men engaging in any sexual activity at all, lying by claiming to be awakened when one is in fact not, and abstaining from alcohol specifically. Would killing your neighbor, stealing their shoes, denying having done so, and smoking a joint then be advisable Buddhist practice? Of course not! The very articulation of these precepts assumed a morality common to a cultural context that did not need to be articulated by a religious community, rather these guidelines were specific to life within a given community and maintaining the harmony thereof by addressing specific issues that had come up from time to time.

It may be easy to understand, then, that these precepts did not have their origin or intention wrapped up in any global significance but with time, and the practice of many, many people over thousands of years has become refined as modes of aware inquiry into our actions and assumptions. At its heart, the practice of these first Five Precepts asks us to pay attention to the fact that we live in a complex web of interdependence with others, wherein the person capable of practicing the dharma is both rare and precious, and where suffering and liberation are universally held. These precepts invite us to realize that all things, not just beings, originate and persist as compounded phenomena and that the best we can really ever do is care well for the things entrusted to us for a time. We're called by the precepts to take note of the significant power that is sexuality, in its ability to forge bonds, yield pleasure, and create life, as in its potential to sow the seeds of suffering, transmit diseases of the body, and mind, and distort thinking. In practicing with these precepts, we're bid to understand the complex nature of reality and in this its ability to be perceived and reflected in ways that work toward aims oppositional to awakening. We're moved in our working with these precepts to value lucidity and the sobriety demanded by keeping in touch with the flow of reality so that we may respond to it in harmonious accord, and thereby not give root to greed, anger, and ignorance.

The second grouping of Five Precepts constituting the Ten Grave Precepts is often translated as follows:

- I vow not to slander.
- I vow not to praise self at the expense of others.
- I vow not to be avaricious.
- I vow not to harbor ill will.
- I vow not to disparage the Three Treasures.

Again, we're directed here even further into a specific, relative application of the common calls of the precepts. We should mind the power of our tongues and beware the tendency to expand and concretize our self-concept (especially in relation to others). We're steered in these precepts toward the realization that greed exists not just in big ways, but in subtle and insidious patterns that can slowly consume us. We are advised to not make permanent the temporal feelings related to the phenomena that we're most prone to cling to (our attitudes toward those who have seemingly wronged us). Finally, these precepts remind us of our preexisting commitments, and to not give up on them when we brush up against them, and not to fall prey to cursing reality when we fall out of step with it.

As is perhaps becoming now readily apparent, the practice of precepts is essentially a process of checking in with reality, undoing our habitual assumptions, wisely stewarding our karmic consequences, and not enlivening errant views of reality. As may already also be clear, precepts are not straightforward injunctions against specific behaviors, and as such they cannot possibly be strictly adhered to or broken with ease, they demand dialectic, contemplative, and ongoing relating. In the ceremonies common to some Zen lineages, instruction is often given during jukai that before the day is out, each of the precepts newly committed to will already be broken. What then are we to do? The Zen paradigm is not one of continual, linear progression and advancement common to other mundane pursuits, rather it is one of amorphous expansion and contraction, defying exacting definitions and movement in the same way reality denies stability and consistency. In this, Zen mirrors reality, again and again.

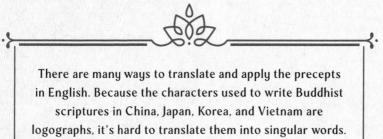

There are many ways to translate and apply the precepts in English. Because the characters used to write Buddhist scriptures in China, Japan, Korea, and Vietnam are logographs, it's hard to translate them into singular words. Research at least several translations of the precepts to get a sense for what is being conveyed in their original context.

Precepts practice and life by vow are methods of intentionally attaining to liberation by means of subscribing to limitations. These limits, though, are but rumble strips on the side of a highway.

They exist to keep the practitioner journeying toward Buddhahood on the well-paved and clear path, not through rails that can only facilitate exact movement along a single track, and not through impassable guard rails, but via clear sounds that serve to alert us to our proximity to the dangers that constitute the shoulder of the road. Should we unintentionally veer off course, the rumble strips gently alert us to correct course, but if we move to intentionally pull off the road, for good or ill, they don't impede our ability to do so.

It is the hope of Zen teachers that precepted students will pull off the road only to aid others who may have strayed or fallen from the path, but indeed all teachers know that new drivers are prone to testing the limits of their vehicles, and even more mature commuters are subject to fits of inattention that in the least interact with the rumble strips of the precepts. Practice does not equate to perfection, it is rather synonymous with intention and attention, the refinement of which can serve to overcome nearly any challenge. This is the practice of precepts. This is life by vow.

A Zen student wearing robes and a rakusu (left) beside their teacher in a Zen Master's traditional robes, no longer wearing the rakusu (right). It should be noted that red robes are (in many traditions) worn by masters and not students, apart from the the Vajrayana sect. The color of the robes and kesa/rakusu is significant in the wider Buddhist community.

COMMITTING
TO THE ZEN BUDDHIST PATH

1. Find a space and time where you can be alone for a few moments. Invite the sacred into that space by placing an image of the Buddha that you find inspiring before you. If you wish you can light candles or offer a stick of incense.

2. Clear your mind and focus on your resolve to commit yourself to the exploration of the enlightened path of the Buddha.

3. Placing your hands in the gassho position (hands held together at chest height, palm to palm, with the fingers pointing upward) recite the Threefold Refuge three times:

   🪷 I take refuge in the Buddha, in awakening itself.

   🪷 I take refuge in the Dharma, the teachings themselves.

   🪷 I take refuge in the Sangha, wise friends too on the path.

4. Offer a slight bow to seal your resolve.

CHAPTER 5

ZEN MEDITATION

Zen is inseparable from meditation. The very word *Zen* is a transliteration of the Chinese word *Chan*, which in turn is derived of the Sanskrit term *Dhyana*, which literally means contemplation or meditation. But meditation is not always a practice synonymous with Buddhism. For many Buddhists, spiritual practice is more a matter of personal piety and devotion to archetypes and deities (such as the Buddha of Infinite Light, *Amitabha*) than it is of meditation. For many other Buddhists, spiritual practice is inseparable from the study and memorization of scripture. It is this form of scholastic practice that was likely predominant by the time of Bodhidharma's arrival at the Shaolin Temple in China, where his teaching concerning the direct realization of the nature of mind and reality took root, named then with the term that most characterized his teaching, that is meditation. Zen meditation is not a generic practice. Not all or even most forms of meditation could rightly be termed Zen. So, what is Zen meditation? The Korean Master Seung Sahn famously taught that Zen meditation is "how you keep your mind, moment after moment." Zen meditation is not about developing extraordinary states, it does not involve complex visualizations, it need not employ any special equipment, and it contains no secrets. Indeed, the secrets of Zen meditation are in plain view for all to see—in the most routine form, simply sit down, quiet down, and pay attention. The fine details of formal seated Zen meditation (or *zazen*) may be broken down into three primary components, namely what to do with the body, what to do with the breath, and what to do with the mind.

CONCERNING THE BODY

The mind follows the body, and the body follows the mind. If our posture is upright and attentive our minds tend to also be awake and aware. Conversely, if our posture is slouched or reclined, our minds tend also to slump and lull. Therefore, the posture of Zen meditation is upright, with the body's weight distributed naturally across the frame, self-supporting and at ease.

While Zen meditation does not require any specialized equipment, often there are specialized implements utilized in Zen training halls by those able to use them, including equipment to meditate in, and equipment to meditate on.

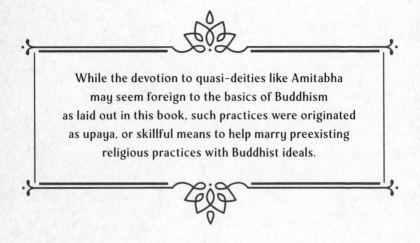

While the devotion to quasi-deities like Amitabha may seem foreign to the basics of Buddhism as laid out in this book, such practices were originated as upaya, or skillful means to help marry preexisting religious practices with Buddhist ideals.

WHAT TO MEDITATE IN

In addition to the rakusu, or token robe, worn by precepted members of many Zen communities, there is other specialized clothing that can be worn by lay students and priests to support the formal practice of Zen meditation. While the various types of clothing and vestments one may encounter are too numerous to list here, it should be noted that Zen meditation is best accomplished in comfortable, relaxed-fit clothing that doesn't bind or constrict, or draw one's somatic attention to too much. In formal Zen practice, it is often recommended that natural-colored, muted-toned, non-patterned clothing be worn (especially in communal practice settings). In Japanese Zen centers, the recommended color is usually black, while in Korean and Vietnamese contexts, gray is often preferred (with robes to be worn over one's daily clothing often being made available to visitors as they enter temples and centers).

While the function of loose-fitting clothing might be rather obvious, the function of muted tones might be less so. In general, it may be understood that during meditation the mind often encounters boredom and will proactively search out any anomaly to make inquiry of, or to build an imaginative reality atop, thereby distracting the meditator from catching a glimpse of the nature of the mind itself (by involving the meditator in endless ado, save for raw perception). Therefore, the simpler the environment and materials within it, the better. Also, commonly plain clothing helps to flatten the socio-economic diversity of the Zen hall (Zendo), allowing practitioners to attend to practice as relative equals. In the Zen dojo (literally "place of the way") sentient beings are all equal and there is no division to be magnified that could otherwise distract from the reality of our interbeing.

WHAT TO MEDITATE ON

Because posture is important in Zen meditation, it is common to see various cushions and mats employed in Zen centers to aid practitioners in assuming sustainable postures that facilitate blood circulation and wakefulness in long periods of seated meditation. Most commonly a small round pillow called a *zafu*, stuffed with buckwheat hulls or kapok fiber, is situated atop a larger rectangular mat called a *zabuton*. These sets of cushions are then arranged either on the floor or on elevated wooden platforms called *tan* in such a way that will allow practitioners to assume a gaze that falls to a wall or toward the floor, unimpeded by other bodies or cushions. While many serious practitioners procure zafu and zabuton for use at home, they are not strictly necessary. Seated Zen practice may also be easily accomplished with a chair.

Having donned loose, neutral clothing, one's attention may naturally fall to just exactly how to hold one's body in seated meditation practice. The general principles that most Zen lineages uphold are that the spine should be held straight, as if the body were suspended from a string affixed to the crown of the head. The natural curvature of the spine should be used as a guide, defining the specific angles at which the body's weight can be supported by the frame with minimal muscular involvement. Tension in the muscles is unsustainable as it leads to both painful cramping and numbness and tingling that will prevent one from focusing on the task at hand and perceiving the very nature of mind and reality; instead, one will be totally preoccupied with the discomfort of their body.

Having situated the spine, it is important to sit with the knees positioned beneath the hips (which is the purpose of the zafu; if practicing on a chair, it is likely that a cushion or other prop will be needed the keep the hips elevated slightly above the knees). In this, the hip flexors are open so as not to constrict blood flow to the lower extremities, with two knees on the zabuton with the buttocks on the zafu, or conversely with the feet flat on the ground if sitting in a chair.

The most common position for the hands is called the *cosmic mudra*, which involves placing the two hands on the lap, at or just beneath the level of the naval so that the weight of the arms falls comfortably onto the frame of the body. The left palm rests in the right, and the tips of the thumbs are brought together to gently touch, thereby forming a circle. If during meditation a practitioner finds themselves with the circle formed by the thumbs having fallen apart, it is likely they've lost diligence and their minds have wandered. Similarly, if one finds themselves forcefully holding the *mudra* or hand form together with much tension and pressure, they have likely drifted from the gentle, penetrating gaze of zazen and entered a phase of cognitive rumination.

A Zen student once asked their teacher for a new mudra, stating that they did not care for the cosmic mudra. The teacher replied, "Okay, no problem," and stretching one hand up and over their back, and one around to the small of their back they continued, "This is your new mudra." The student responded, "Thank you very much, I think I'll keep the cosmic mudra!" The forms of Zen have been perfected over many years, and while accommodations can be made for physical ability, Zen practice is no place for the machinations of small likes and dislikes.

ZEN MEDITATION POSITIONS (ZAZEN)

FULL LOTUS

HALF LOTUS

QUARTER LOTUS

BURMESE

SEIZA WITH BENCH

SEIZA WITH CHAIR

CONCERNING
THE BREATH

Breath is the liminal space, or connective tissue, that unifies the body and mind. Breath is a sacred function that is at once autonomic and unconscious. Should we ignore the breath or fall asleep, it finds its own rhythms and accords with the conditions both inside and outside of the body. Should we seek to consciously speed up, slow down, elongate, or shorten our breath, we can do so with the most subtle passing of thought. Breath is both a function of mind and body at once. Therefore, both mind and body follow the breath, and the breath follows body and mind. If our breath is well tended to, deep and rhythmic, our minds and bodies will be relaxed, also tending to the natural rhythms of reality. If our breath is shallow and quick, our bodies and minds will also be unsettled and engaged in topical perception.

Generally speaking, the breath of Zen meditation is relaxed, yet metered and deep. Preferably taking place through the nose for both inhalation and exhalation, breathing in zazen engages the belly and diaphragm, allowing the lungs to fully inflate and thereby supply sufficient oxygen to the bloodstream, ensuring that the brain is not panicked and is operating at its highest possible capacity. Ideally, the exhalation lasts twice as long as the inhalation, and all but the gentlest of tension is exerted upon the abdominal muscles to facilitate this controlled breathing pattern.

Physically, the position of the knees (being situated beneath the hips) works to open space for the lower abdomen to fully expand with one's inhalation, and to gently collapse with exhalation. The cosmic mudra provides a physical reference for the proper exercise of *tanden soku,* Zen's specific form of diaphragmatic, abdominal breathing.

While each Zen lineage tends to have idiosyncratic instruction for the exacting methods of breath control in zazen, a beginning student can be sufficiently situated in the practice through breathing in such a way that one's belly might expand through the opening of the mudra if not for the belly reaching its natural apex with the full inflation of the lungs, and thereby demanding a gentle collapse with the exhalation.

CONCERNING THE MIND

Once again it should be said that mind follows body and body follows mind (and don't forget about breath!). Fundamentally, there is no separation between the mind and body, and it is only in relative terms that we divide the real into constituent parts for focused examination. In reality, mind and body must be realized as one, and that one must be perceived as part of an even greater one, the body–mind of reality itself, both manifest and latent. If one's mind is racing or disturbed, it is likely that one's body will reflect this, with posture and breath suffering at the mind's expense, in all but the most seasoned of practitioners.

It is easy to confuse zazen as an activity primarily wrapped up with the function of the mind alone. This is an errant view, however. It has been said that Zen enters through the body and not the mind, but the opposite is also sometimes true, seeing as in reality the body and mind are not two. Nonetheless, we cannot hope to tend to the mind without tending to the body, nor to tend to the mind without manifesting such tending in the body.

When one first assumes the posture of zazen the mind may be initially amused and intrigued with the novelty of the practice. In short order, though, the mind tends to become familiar with the situation and thus tries to occupy its attention elsewhere. In the Zen hall, despite the initial mystique, there is very little to occupy the mind. Speaking is limited, if not entirely absent, movement is kept to a minimum, and the sound of silence can become amplified to nearly deafening levels; light is dimmed, color is muted, and commonly the scent of incense quickly fades into the background. In such an environment, the mind is left with little but itself in short measure, and it will throw utter fits to escape the seeming solitude of introspection, lest the secret of its fundamental insubstantiality be made known to the egoic identity that otherwise narrates its reality.

Zen's answer to the mind's initial antics in the practice of zazen is often an initial capacity-building exercise known as *susokukan*, or breath counting. In this exercise, as the posture of zazen is assumed, beginning students will be instructed in various ways to focus their attention on their breathing, perhaps numbering on each cycle of inhalation and exhalation, from one to ten, and perhaps even from ten to one. When the mind is found to have drifted from its assigned preoccupation with counting, be it with the task of psychically ringing the bell to end the meditation period or with the certainty that the garage door has been left open at home to disastrous consequence, the meditator simply begins again, at one.

By the time sufficient concentration (or as the mind may otherwise frame it, resignation) has been built so as to allow the practitioner to complete a full cycle of counting, one's teacher may begin moving their practice into specific directions to encourage them to catch a fuller and fuller glimpse of the mind's very nature, and reality itself non-distinct from that.

While Zen meditation is not generic, it is also not as specific as some mindfulness methods (like contemporary Vipassana practice). Because Zen is a living tradition, the actual details of Zen meditation practice may evolve over time with instruction differing from teacher to teacher and person to person. Meditation isn't the end game, it's but a mode of practice moving one toward awakening.

The purpose of Zen meditation is that of Zen Buddhism itself. As captured in the first two chapters of the present text, Zen is a process of awakening from the slumber of our conceptions, via awareness and acceptance. Awakening into the fullness of reality as it is, we may begin to respond in harmonious accord with reality, and thereby allay our suffering, which is primarily understood as the tension and friction that exists between reality as it is conceived and reality as it may be perceived. The practice of Zen meditation seeks to bridge the chasm of understanding and experience by laying both a foundational conceptual framework to bound from, and establishing a practice by which to bound, leaving then the place to bound (reality itself) to its own devices, knowing that the introduction to the seeming "other shore" (of reality) is nothing short of a homecoming. In this homecoming, the seeming self finds that in actuality it has never even had the option of leaving home and that all has been in harmony all along. It is with this very realization that one enters the most advanced form of practice-realization known as *shikantaza*, or silent illumination.

Shikantaza is ultimately relegated neither to silence or sound, stillness or motion, standing or sitting, or even illumination or obfuscation. But alas, words fail to do much but infer, to point us in the general direction of the experience that they hope to convey. Call it silent illumination or cacophonous darkness, the direct experience and manifestation of the all-enveloping fabric of reality as untorn despite the machinations of our small-minded thinking is what is meant by shikantaza, and in shikantaza, practice and the fruits of its realization themselves merge. This is the manner of life assumed by Zen masters and the aspiration of all sincere practitioners.

En route to the realization and manifestation of shikantaza, numerous practice modalities may be engaged in the container of zazen, including koankufu, the famed wrestling with Zen's case studies into the nature of the awakened mind (*koans*), which number into the thousands. In the following chapter, the practice of koankufu will be examined in some depth and, by its very nature, more will be revealed concerning the practice and progression of practice in zazen.

BUILDING A DAILY MEDITATION PRACTICE

As you have learned in this chapter, Zen Buddhist meditation is a relatively simple matter. Sit down, quiet down, and pay attention—that's it. Of course, fine details about posture and breath exist in the Zen tradition to help us maximize our efforts, and not be overly distracted or deterred by the sensations and inclinations of the body.

While the particulars of meditation could be explored for many months, or even years, there is no time like the present to get started in this practice. One need not sit for the typical 30 to 40-minute periods of an established Zen practice; even 5 or 10 minutes practiced with daily resolve can firmly set one on the path of awakening. The key is consistency.

- When starting a meditation practice, it's best to do so for the same amount of time, at approximately the same time every day. Having a more malleable or flexible schedule lends itself to procrastination and exceptions that will no doubt complicate the establishment of the practice.

- Find some time in the morning, or early evening, when you are not yet physically exhausted from the day, and your mental faculties can still be directed with wakeful intention.

- While you can procure the specialized meditation cushions (zafu and zabuton) described in this chapter, you can also simply sit in a straight back chair.

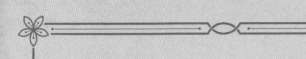

1. Sitting centered and upright with three points of contact (either your behind and two knees on a cushion, or two flat feet and your behind in a chair), assume the cosmic mudra (fingers of left hand cradling the fingers of your right hand, tips of thumbs touching), and take a moment to scan your body for any signs of excessive muscle tension, or discomfort. Relax into your posture, allowing the body to be supported by its frame to the fullest extent possible.

2. Take several deep breaths, fully opening the lungs, pressing down the diaphragm, and expanding the belly on the inhalation to prime your breathing, and again, check your posture to make sure you are in proper alignment for further tandensoku (abdominal breathing).

3. Begin you meditation with the practice of susokukan (breath counting), breathing in and out from the lower abdomen, and focusing your mind on counting each cycle, from one to ten. If you reach five, or perhaps even two and find your mind distracted, simply note that, and return to your mindful breathing. Gradually you will find that your capacity for focusing your attention will increase, and you will be able to mindfully follow your breath for ten or even twenty cycles (continuing in reverse from ten to one). This is a practice that can take a considerable amount of time to develop though—be gentle on yourself but remain committed to the practice.

Meditation will be further explored in additional exercises throughout this book. For now, though, the practice of susokukan and tandensoku is ideal and preferred.

CHAPTER 6

ZEN KOANS: CASE STUDIES IN AWAKENING

The koan is perhaps the most famed and most misunderstood aspect of Zen Buddhist practice. Often mistakenly described as riddles that are intended to stunt the conceptual mind of the student and expedite their entry into a state of non-thinking, koans are mistranslated as often as they are misunderstood. Commonly, for instance, one may hear a famous koan summarized as "what is the sound of one hand clapping?" To this, casual and clever observers may try to flap one of their hands around attempting to make a sound. Others will mime clapping to the air, noting that there is no sound. Still others simply grin, as if such silent amusement could possibly be the point. In reality, the famed Zen master Hakuin Ekaku actually posited that "when two hands clap there is a sound; what is the sound of the single hand?" Again, what is the sound of the single hand? This is the question that a keen-eyed Zen student would seek to enter into, become one with, and then be able to respond to with clarity.

The word koan is a compound term, composed of two characters (公案) which literally mean "public case," in the sense of case law, or a case study. In essence, koans are simply recorded interactions between great Zen masters and their students, monks and enlightened shopkeepers, and in more than one case, elderly women giving scripture masters the how-to. Koans are only paradoxical or riddling to the uninitiated, after all, they are case studies into the nature of the awakened mind, being exercised in the course of relatively normal life. Through deeply examining these records of awakening in practice, it is hoped that Zen students will be able to catch a glimpse of the view that they portray, not merely as another rule to an ever-evolving cognitive framework, but as a feeling and as a spark that can ignite the latent enlightened potential that Buddhism postulates is possessed by all sentient beings.

PRACTICING WITH KOANS

Koan practice, or koankufu (literally, extreme devotion to the case study), is a dialectical task. Like all things in the practice of Zen, a teacher is ultimately the director of koan practice, and while different lineages mean that people begin the practice of koans at different points, it is generally understood that a student should be conversant with the basic philosophy and teaching of Zen Buddhism, and well-enough practiced in Zen meditation so as to sufficiently hold the case in meditative view, as an extension of zazen. Once a teacher has determined that a student is prepared to begin (and is otherwise well suited to the task of) the practice of koan introspection, they will privately assign a specific case for a student to carry into the meditation practice and daily life.

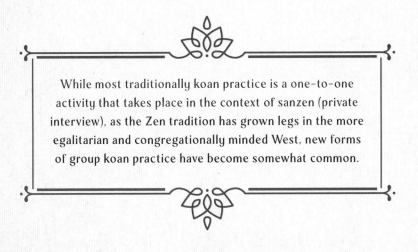

While most traditionally koan practice is a one-to-one activity that takes place in the context of sanzen (private interview), as the Zen tradition has grown legs in the more egalitarian and congregationally minded West, new forms of group koan practice have become somewhat common.

Koan practice is at once an extension of one's meditation practice (zazen) and of the practice of meeting privately with the teacher to receive specific guidance on one's spiritual cultivation (sanzen). Koan introspection is a private practice between the teacher and student and is not to be otherwise shared or discussed outside of that relationship until such a time that a student may be entrusted as a duly qualified teacher and lineage holder themselves. The purpose for privacy around this practice is multifaceted. On one hand, while formally recorded koans number well into the thousands, it is typical for the curriculum or *shitsunai* of a particular lineage to involve several hundred cases. While this may seem like a large number, it is likely that students in any given practice center will be working on common cases at one time. In this, it is possible that in discussing koan practice with other students, the direction of any of the conversing students' practice could be disrupted, derailed, or otherwise short-circuited, lest they be handed a view that is best arrived at through organic realization. The Western adage about teaching someone to fish, versus giving them a fish applies here.

Koankufu often deals with themes of the utmost existential significance, and care must be exercised when working with these themes with the intensity demanded of formal koan practice to safeguard the mental and spiritual wellbeing of the students. Therefore, this practice falls within the specific purview of expert teachers and their qualified students. That said, the practice can be discussed generally without ill effect—specifics are what is to be safeguarded.

Once a koan has been assigned to a student, in the most classical training method the initial task of the student is to memorize the case word for word. While some cases are quite brief, many others are quite long, as records of narrative and dialogue sometimes spanning multiple page lengths. After the assignment of a koan, a student will be met in sanzen by their teacher with the increasingly familiar question of "what is your practice?" To this, the student would respond by literally presenting the case from memory. In the strictest practice settings, if a single word is missed or if the student falters in their delivery, the teacher will simply ring a small handbell, signifying that the interview has come to an end, and that the student should return to their meditation cushion and continue to familiarize themselves with the koan. There is no question, no protestation, or option at this point but to retreat, be it with disappointment, frustration, or even relief.

The purpose of memorizing a koan is to essentially ensure that the student can become one with the case and hold it clearly in their mind's eye to realize in formal meditation practice or in the course of one's daily life. If the case is not part of the student, the student cannot become part of the case, and the awakened vision to which the koan points will remain as a story rather than as a reality in which the student takes part and carries forth. That said, in many Western practice environments it is no longer a standard practice to require a student to fully memorize a case before proceeding with the practice pertaining to it. To many contemporary Zen masters a paraphrase of the case is sufficient, with some traditions simply requiring students to read the assigned case in printed form. While in some ways this is certainly more efficient, it is arguable that the practice suffers when more cursory attention is given to the case itself, with full focus then shifted to merely *figuring it out*.

When it happens that a student is able to present their assigned case in sanzen to the teacher's satisfaction with regards to both content and demeanor, the practice progresses with the teacher inquiring as to the student's understanding and realization of the koan. Here again, the style will vary from lineage to lineage and teacher to teacher, but in general, koankufu is not about discursive analysis or literary critique. Students who launch into diatribes about what they think the case means will likely be swiftly dismissed by the sound of the bell, beckoned back to their bewildered holding of the case in practice, brushing up against uncertainty and unknowing in equal measure, perhaps even to the point of despair. It is very often in this place of persistence mingling with despair that one meets the edges of their cleverness, and they can then experience the koan rather than continue to merely analyze the case. From this, a meaningful response may be summoned, often spontaneously, that a teacher will be able to wholeheartedly affirm.

It often happens that the initial affirmation of a teacher comes in the form of checking questions that probe the student's response for its sincerity, specificity, and congruence with the wisdom of a given lineage. These questions are at times met with worthy responses, one after another. And at other times, the initial excitement at the lack of an immediate bell toll is often short-lived, as one finds their center and certainty utterly disrupted by a turning word, glance, or inquiry by the teacher, and it's back to the cushion. Eventually, though, a student breaks through and manifests the wisdom gleaned through partaking in the view intrinsic to the experience of a given koan. At this point a student may be passed on the case and assigned another—passed and given instructions for appendant ancillary practices, or in the most traditional way tasked with finding a capping phrase, or *jakugo*, to encapsulate their realization. The practice of appending jakugo to cases, while completely common in Asia, is relatively uncommon in the West. In reality, there is much to the traditional koan practice that is wrapped up with ancient East Asian culture that is linguistically and culturally unavailable to all but the most erudite of keen-eyed students. In some Western practice centers, students are asked to compose their own jakugo when the practice is not entirely omitted.

In East Asia, koan practice often comprises not just a method of meditative inquiry, but also a manner of formal education. In the days before Western-style universities and Buddhist seminaries, the scholastic rigor demanded by koan practice included the ability to read and understand ancient Chinese characters, familiarity with spiritual literature and cultural classics, alongside the lore of multiple groups of people. This academic formation came to a head in its application in the practice of appending jakugo to cases otherwise sufficiently digested. In modern times, this practice has become more rote in Asia (with monastic students often receiving small guidance texts as a matter of regular course), and frankly unnecessary in Western contexts, which accounts for the delay in the translation of the materials and the transplanting of the practice. With the progression through the full koan curriculum (shitsunai) of most lineages often taking around twenty years of regular engagement, students certainly have their work cut out for them and are set for a lifetime of practice in the absence of jakugo practice, let alone with its inclusion.

Due to the patriarchal nature of the ancient world, most major koan collections are comprised of cases of male monks working toward enlightenment. Interestingly though, when women make an appearance in these classical collections, they often stump these very monks or offer turning words that lead otherwise eminent teachers to more profound understandings.

CASES FOR CONSIDERATION

There are two primary koan collections that are common to most every lineage that employs the practice of koankufu, often forming the base of every shitsunai, namely the forty-eight cases of the Gateless Gate (or *Mumonkan*) and the one hundred cases of the Blue Cliff Record (or *Hekiganroku*). From here lineages will often veer off into idiosyncratic curriculums of often hundreds of other cases, which may be examined in the order presented in the compilations, or in an order unique to the temple or even to the student. Most of these collections, including the Gateless Gate collection and the Blue Cliff Record, are widely available in many translations, often with formal commentaries (or *teisho*) written by preeminent teachers included. It is in this format that koans are most commonly publicly discussed. While these formal commentaries may indeed elucidate a proper view of the case that they concern, the experience of working with a koan in sanzen remains distinct from that which can be gleaned from their public analysis. Nonetheless, interested readers can find these collections and benefit from them, engaging them as a form of literature or even scripture.

That said, caution is warranted in coming to any fixed or authoritative views of the cases.

In the following pages, five cases from the famous koan collection known as the Mumonkan will be presented with brief commentary, intended to make clear the examination of koans as a practice both central and unique to the Zen Buddhist tradition.

JOSHU'S BOWL (CASE 7)

A monk once approached master Joshu saying,
"I have just entered the monastery. Please teach me." Joshu responded,
"Have you eaten your breakfast?" "I have," said the monk.
Joshu replied, saying, "Then go wash your bowl."
At this, the monk was awakened.

COMMENTARY: Zen puts forward that awakened life is not distinct from the ordinariness of day-to-day living. Often we get so caught up in our longings for escape from our suffering, that we combine liberation from suffering with the transcendence of the experience of daily life. In this case, a new monk in seemingly just such a state renounced his life as he had known it, and entered the monastery (little known to him, an institution that concentrates and magnifies the fullness of ordinary life into a microcosm, rather than offering an alternative to it). Approaching the spiritual director Joshu, this monk, while clearly already engaged in the daily rhythm of the monastery while yet casting it as unrelated to the task of awakening, asks for instruction. Joshu, not ignoring the monk's request for spiritual direction, instructs the monk to continue to align himself with the demands of the moment: having eaten, wash your bowls!

How often do we allow our stories about life, and about our suffering in particular, to grow legs of their own, and supersede reality? The enlightenment of the new monk in this case did not come after years of endless practice but rather with a moment of awareness, as his errant perspective was reflected back to him in such a way that he could return to his life already in progress, responding in harmonious accord to all that there was to be aware and in acceptance of.

TOZAN'S THREE POUNDS (CASE 18)

One day while he was at work weighing some flax, a monk approached Tozan and asked, "What is Buddha?" Tozan responded by saying, "This flax weighs three pounds."

COMMENTARY: Zen is always about just this very moment, in just this very place. In waking up we open our eyes, not to the world of dreams, but to the world of actuality. Do you see? Do you hear? What is so very wrong about this precise moment? Setting aside our stories for a time we may realize that it is just their weight that is at the root of our grief. Remembering that wultimately Buddha is but a metaphor for reality, a monk asked Tozan about just that—"Master, what is real?" "Just this, just this," the Tozan replied.

NOT THE WIND, NOT THE FLAG (CASE 29)

Two monks were arguing about a flag, one asserting,
"It is the flag that is moving!" the other countering,
"Surely it is the wind that is moving!"
Hearing this, the sixth Patriarch Huineng admonished them both.
"It is not the wind, nor the flag that is moving—
your minds are moving!"

COMMENTARY: Two monks, two minds, two visions of what's real. Enter then the master Huineng, and all of a sudden appear three monks, three minds, and three visions of what's real. Is it the wind, the flag, or the mind? If you ask me, what's in motion is motion. Indeed, we're all prone to getting caught up in false dichotomies and faux dilemmas. It's not that rumination isn't worthwhile, endless innovation has been born of daydreaming. But do we know we're dreaming when we're dreaming? In conflict and confrontation do we have true agency? This case isn't about being right or wrong, indeed all three visions have their rationales, strengths, and weaknesses. Huineng entered the dialogue with this awareness and thus agency, while the two monks were stuck in their respective certainty, unable to get out of their rut without a tow.

JOSHU'S OAK TREE IN THE GARDEN (CASE 38)

A monk once asked Master Joshu,
"Why did Bodhidharma come to China?" Joshu responded saying,
"The oak tree in the garden."

COMMENTARY: If Buddha is ultimately a metaphor for reality, Bodhidharma's journey to the east could be nothing less—after all, what more could he have to impart? Again and again, Zen is only about what's real, and about what's now. Life doesn't pause when we check out in rumination; Joshu, knowing this, invited the monk back to the clicking of a keyboard and the gentle hum of an air conditioner, Bodhidharma's enduring message known well to this author.

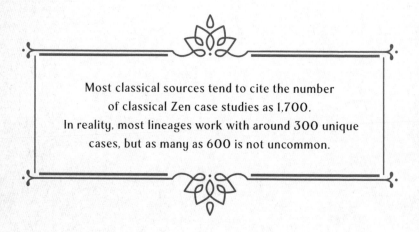

Most classical sources tend to cite the number
of classical Zen case studies as 1,700.
In reality, most lineages work with around 300 unique
cases, but as many as 600 is not uncommon.

A HUNDRED-FOOT POLE (CASE 46)

Sekiso once asked, "How can you proceed from the top of a hundred-foot pole?" A Zen teacher responded, "One who sits atop a hundred-foot pole has attained a certain height but has still not realized Zen's depths! They should proceed from there, and manifest in the world in ten directions!"

COMMENTARY: The teaching that set the wheel of dharma into motion, establishing the Buddhist path, was that of non-self. When the self is realized as insubstantial, where does its apparent form go? It has been said that no meaning is great meaning, and therefore it may be understood that non-self is omni-self. One's true body indeed fills the ten directions, and for the adept at the height of realization, one more step is necessary. This doesn't mean to die, though it does mean to let go. But into what? At the beginning of this chapter, we learned of Hakuin's asking, "What is the sound of the single hand clapping?" A prolific artist, he painted many portraits of a single hand thrust freely into space. One should ponder, do these paintings make any sound?

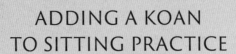

ADDING A KOAN
TO SITTING PRACTICE

After one has gained a sufficiently stable practice and developed enough concentration with the practice of tandensoku and susokukan, there are numerous methods that may be interjected into one's meditation practice by a competent spiritual director. One of those potential practices is koankufu, working with Zen's famed case studies in awakening.

<ul>
<li>This chapter offers five koan cases for your consideration, alongside some comments that offer pointers to significant aspects of each case. For this exercise, peruse these koans, and find one that piques your interest. In the most traditional way, you might devote some time to memorizing the case verbatim so that you could recite it back on command, word for word. Working with the case in this way makes it an aspect of your mind, rather than an external object to be engaged.</li>

<li>Once the case has been memorized, the task becomes working with it with some fervor, both inside and outside of meditation. Keep the case at the periphery of your day, and at the center of your attention in meditation, don't let it escape your consideration.</li>

<li>A primary method of working with a koan is to attempt to become one with it, or to enter into it. Pay attention to what feelings and sensations arise in your holding of the koan in your conscious awareness. The job here is not understanding but experiencing.</li>
</ul>

You may find that after some time, the koan will open up for you in considerable ways. Where there was heaviness and unknowing, there may then be levity and an attainment of the case wherein its wisdom is unlocked and incorporated into your experience and life as a whole. These experiences are ideally processed with a teacher, but if no teacher is available, or you're finding yourself content to practice as a solo practitioner, move on to another case, either from this book or from one of the traditional collections. Take time, don't rush, and don't run away from the discomfort of unknowing, always lean into it.

In the West, the most common lineages often introduce study via an initial koan that is explored with up to a couple hundred questions. From there, the 48 koans of the Gateless Gate collection (the Mumonkan) and the 100 Koans of the Blue Cliff Record (the Hekiganroku) are commonly engaged. Following this, collections, such as the 272 cases of the Entangling Vines (Shumon Kattoshu), may be traversed, or the 100 cases of the Book of Serenity (the Shoyoroku), or the assorted cases of the Record of the Transmission of the Lamp (the Denkoroku). Finally, the 16 precepts are often engaged as koans, along with Master Dongshan's Five Ranks. As you can see, there is plenty of material to inform a lifetime of study, and it is not uncommon for formal koan practice under the watchful direction of a competent teacher to take twenty or more years to complete.

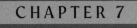

CHAPTER 7

STUDY
AS A PATH OF
ZEN PRACTICE

In the first chapter of this book, we learned that the foundational parameters of Zen as given by Bodhidharma establish it as a path of awakening clearly transmitted "outside of the scriptures" without "dependence on words and letters." In the preceding chapter on koankufu, though, we also learned that the practice of koans essentially served as a path of scholastic education for monks and priests of the Zen school in premodern times. One may then ask, which is it? It's important to remember that scholasticism has been an aspect of Buddhism since its earliest days, when before the widespread adoption of writing, Buddhist monks would gather and collectively recite the words of the Buddha so as to preserve and study them. That's not to say that study and scholasticism are inherently Zen practice forms, but it is to note that they are not inherently contradictory paths either.

It is true that the history of Zen contains several famous stories pertaining to sutra-come-Zen masters like Tokusan burning his commentaries on the *Diamond Sutra*, having exhausted his understanding when meeting with the Zen teacher Ryutan, and Daie burning the printing blocks of his teacher Engo's *magnum opus* the *Hekiganroku* (Blue Cliff Record) after deciding that students had become too dependent on conceptual thought, so much so that it was impeding their practice. And looking closely at such accounts we can come to understand that the problem, just as Bodhidharma put it, is in the dependence on words and letters, that is, regarding scripture and written teaching so highly that we begin to depend on it intrinsically as if it could manifest a direct experience of, and ongoing accord with reality for us. Subsequent to Bodhidharma (who himself is attributed as author to a number of sermons and treatises, in addition to the so-called sacred verse of Zen), a great many realized Zen teachers have written books and commentaries, regularly delivered dharma talks and public addresses, and indeed engaged in dialogue with their students to lead them into the direct experience of awakening. Words and letters aren't a problem, utter reliance on them at the expense of the pursuit of direct experience is.

THE NATURE
OF THE MIND IN PRACTICE

How then do Zen practitioners make use of study as a path of practice? An age-old, and certainly well-known Zen analogy puts forward that all teaching is as a finger pointing toward the moon. Whereas the moon represents reality itself, the finger and its pointing represent the teachings, and the direct view of the moon, brought into focus through following the pointing of the finger, represents awakening. In this image, it is to be understood that the finger, or the teachings in their various iterations, must not be conflated with reality nor awakening in the same way that the description or picture of a meal on a restaurant menu should not be assumed to satiate hunger. Rather one must order the meal, apply utensils to it, bring it to one's mouth, chew, and swallow.

Zen teachings are as much of a potential stumbling block as they are endlessly valuable maps leading to the treasure that is the end of suffering and agency in the creation and stewardship of meaning. It is not that the teachings are stumbling blocks unto themselves, however, they are stumbling blocks when they encounter the defense mechanisms of the mind. Western cultural wisdom, especially as pioneered by Sigmund Freud, holds that the mind exists in both conscious and unconscious parts, and the conscious part (or ego) is constantly being pulled between the demands of the primal mind (or id) and those of the situationally informed moderating component of the mind (the superego). Within the structure, it may be understood that the mind is most comfortable operating without a working awareness of the unconscious. Zen Buddhist training, though, tends to elucidate the mind as a whole, composed of its unconscious and conscious parts. It is against this that the mind tends to rebel, casting the teachings themselves as a deep-enough revelation into the nature of reality, personally uninformed and unexperienced as they may be.

Here an analogy may be drawn from the film *The Wizard of Oz*, wherein we can note that the mind likes to operate with conscious awareness only of the large, green, smoke-and-flame-flanked image of Oz as its fundamental unit. When Toto pulls back the curtain, revealing Oz to be but a mirage fueled and controlled by yet-unknown mechanisms dreamt up by a comparatively small and frightened man, the whole system risked coming apart. Making eye contact with Dorothy and her party, the man continues to speak through Oz's microphone-enhanced booming voice, turning a dial that seems to make the whole thing work—"Pay no attention to the man behind the curtain!" Once the attention had been paid, though, there was no going back, and the whole system *did* come apart.

But after that initial shock, experienced by all involved, truth was revealed and with it a way home. In awakening from the dream that had ultimately comprised all but the entirety of the story, Dorothy finds herself among the family and friends whom she'd journeyed alongside all along, now, though, informed by a totally different suffering and ameliorating understanding.

Zen is a pursuit that is about one very specific thing, namely, awakening. Awakening may be understood as an awareness and acceptance of reality that facilitates a harmonious accord with its continual unfolding, both externally and internally.

At numerous junctures in Zen training, we will reveal to ourselves knowledge of the inner workings and constituent parts of our minds. We risk, and indeed endeavor to bring to conscious awareness, the reality that not only is Oz as we've otherwise known him, but smoke and mirrors, and also that the man behind the curtain is but a temporal union of flesh and bone, carbon, oxygen, hydrogen, and nitrogen, waves and particles assembled for a time with no permanent center around which to form and persist. This isn't an entirely safe or comfortable awareness. It's disorienting, upsetting, and outside of the control of the mechanisms that have propelled the mirage of our substantiality forward for this long. Perhaps most importantly, it's unfamiliar, and its territory is unknown, and the only thing more frightening to the mind and disruptive of its long-suffering systems than knowing how things actually are, is not knowing how to respond to them, or to be in the wake of their awareness. Thus, the mind rebels, and encourages us to accept whatever dim light we may encounter as the full brightness of the moon reflecting the sun, and to be satiated with as little disruption as possible. Awakening, though, is only to be had in the fullness of disruption, wherein reorientation can be had and made, and life in accord with how things actually are can then be engaged.

In the Zen vein, study and scholasticism is associated with refuge in the dharma—the teachings themselves, that is, the map to reality that itself is part and parcel to reality, fully a part of it, but not the fullest part of it. Without a map, one risks not really knowing or being oriented to the destination, and wandering in the dark endlessly. The teachings are essential, but they are not themselves the journey. Thus, as Bodhidharma taught, should they be engaged; attainment, after all, is not to be found in the direct pointing, but in the direct looking at what is being pointed out, whereby we can become Buddha.

ZEN SCRIPTURES

The canon of Buddhism is not fixed in the same way as many religions; it remains open, either overtly or subtly, and has functioned that way since the time of Buddha Shakyamuni's passing. The earliest Buddhist scriptures were simply the communally recollected and preserved teachings of Shakyamuni Buddha. These collected teachings are known in the wider Buddhist world as the Tripitaka (or the Three Baskets), consisting of the Buddha's teachings on the path to the cessation of suffering (Sutra Pitaka), the Buddha's guidance for the day-to-day lives of monks and priests (Vinaya Pitaka), and the so-called higher teachings (Abhidhamma Pitaka). Interestingly, Buddhist tradition holds that the Abhidhamma Pitaka was given by the Buddha shortly after his own awakening, but then lesser teachings had to be articulated so as to be more accessible to the masses (the contents of the Sutra Pitaka), thereby establishing a foundation by which one could bind to the insights contained in the Abidhamma Pitaka. Conversely, the insights of modern scholarship understand the Abhidhamma Pitaka to be later commentaries on the Buddha's original teachings and the natural expansion of them as they were explored and applied in the wake of the Buddha's life, often in cultural contexts outside of those that received his original dispensations. Therefore, from the very beginning, the Buddhist canon was both open and closed based on the stories told around its contents.

THE HEART SUTRA

While the Zen tradition certainly respects the teachings of the Tripitaka, those scriptures primarily are employed by the Theravada school, though their insights fill the veins of all Buddhist traditions. What is common to all Zen schools, outside of the koan collections, is a firm rooting in the teachings of a relatively brief scripture known as the Heart Sutra. This scripture is chanted every day, sometimes multiple times per day, in nearly every Zen temple, center, or gathering around the world.

Consisting of just fourteen verses in Sanskrit, and two hundred and sixty characters in Chinese, the Heart Sutra conveys the most succinct pointing to the fullness of reality that has perhaps ever been articulated, from a Buddhist perspective. Indeed, it is succinct enough to be included in its complete form here:

Avalokitesvara Bodhisattva
when practicing deeply the Prajna Paramita
perceives that all five skandhas are empty
and is saved from all suffering and distress.
Shariputra, form does not differ from emptiness,
emptiness does not differ from form.
That which is form is emptiness, that which is emptiness form.
The same is true of feelings, perceptions, impulses, and consciousness.
Shariputra, all dharmas are marked with emptiness;
they do not appear or disappear,
are not tainted or pure,
do not increase or decrease.

Therefore, in emptiness there is no form,
no feelings, perceptions, impulses, or consciousness.
No eyes, no ears, no nose, no tongue, no body, no mind;
no color, no sound, no smell, no taste, no touch, no object of mind;
no realm of eyes and so forth until no realm of mind consciousness.
No ignorance and also no extinction of it,
and so forth until no old age and death and also no extinction of them.
No suffering, no origination, no stopping, no path, no cognition,
also no attainment with nothing to attain.
The Bodhisattva depends on Prajna Paramita and the mind
is no hindrance;
without any hindrance no fears exist.
Far apart from every perverted view one dwells in Nirvana.
In the three worlds all Buddhas depend on Prajna Paramita
and attain Anuttara Samyak Sambodhi.
Therefore know that Prajna Paramita is the great transcendent mantra,
is the great bright mantra, is the utmost mantra, is the supreme mantra
which is able to relieve all suffering and is true, not false.
So proclaim the Prajna Paramita mantra,
proclaim the mantra which says:
gate gate paragate parasamgate bodhi svaha.

While there is no doubt that a cursory reading of the Heart Sutra can prove both mystifying and complex, when broken down and examined its message is quite simple, profound, and to the point, while also lending itself the expansion into nearly infinite volumes of commentary and interpretation.

Fundamentally this scripture teaches us that all of reality, as it can be perceived and otherwise labeled, is empty—that is, insubstantial and not capable of holding up under philosophical or scientific scrutiny when examined closely. Understanding this and realizing it in our direct experience is at the heart of awakening and the dissolution of suffering. That said, this emptiness is what mysteriously gives rise to form, and the manifest nature of things that we otherwise see, hear, smell, taste, and touch. Emptiness and form are non-different, just as waves and particles, and from their free interplay all things seemingly arise and seemingly collapse into. So, in reality, there is no real movement, no coming or going, no increasing or decreasing, no purity or taint. Things just are as they are, on both the microcosmic and macrocosmic levels, applying equally to quantum physics and personal psychology. There is nothing really to do, no one to be or become, nothing to attain, and no one to attain it. This awareness itself is freedom—nirvana, and the realization of all Buddhas.

While this scripture and the brief explication above may still prove mind-boggling, the practice of Zen is to keep engaging it, time and time again, in hope that its pointing may be subtly and suddenly realized in the midst of our daily lives and bring about an end to our suffering. Zen practitioners chant this scripture time and time again throughout their lives, priming their mental faculties for its recognition in reality, which is an experience far greater than words can convey, and which words can only allude to.

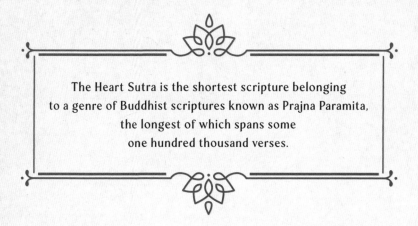

The Heart Sutra is the shortest scripture belonging
to a genre of Buddhist scriptures known as Prajna Paramita,
the longest of which spans some
one hundred thousand verses.

There are a handful of other scriptures, quite longer than the Heart Sutra, which are common to the Zen school, such as the Diamond Sutra, the Mahaparinirvana Sutra, the Lotus Sutra, and the Flower Ornament Sutra (this last scripture being Zen's equivalent to the Abhidhamma Pitaka). Each of these scriptures uses different words, images, and allusions to describe elements of the awakened view that may have not yet even entered our cognitive framework as potentials, all with the intention of priming and preparing us for the dawning of that awakened vision.

Zen does not actually condemn the mental faculties or scholastic pursuits. Instead, it hopes to harness them toward the aim of awakening itself, just not at the expense of practices such as zazen, koankufu, and rites and rituals of practice life that work to bridge mind to body, and the mind-body to reality in harmonious accord, which will be examined in some depth in the next chapter.

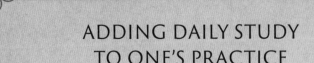

ADDING DAILY STUDY
TO ONE'S PRACTICE

The practice of studying, commenting upon, and even vigorously debating the scriptures and classics of the Buddhist tradition has always been an aspect of Zen practice. Like in learning to drive, at first one needs to pay close attention to traffic signs, lights, and the various arrays of painted lines on the roads. Eventually, though, the knowledge of these things becomes so integrated into one's experience that they no longer demand constant conscious engagement. So too is the practice of studying the scriptures and literature of the tradition.

🪷 For this practice, try adding ten minutes per day of reading from the literature of and about the tradition, either before or after your daily meditation practice. The Zen canon is still open, and the amount of material to be digested is nearly infinite according to one's own karmic propensities. Explore broadly but try not to get caught up in the trap of imaginative practice, always bring what you are reading and studying back to your very experience in the moment.

🪷 Working regularly with the Heart Sutra can be a good bounding point, followed by classics such as the Diamond Sutra, the Platform Sutra, alongside more modern works published by contemporary authors.

ADDING ARTISTIC EXPRESSION
TO ONE'S PRACTICE

There are numerous artistic expressions that share Zen concerns, or that cross over into the realization of Zen in specific ways, that can be engaged by practitioners at every level. For instance, in many Zen temples, *sutra* copying or *shakyo* is a practice that priests and lay people alike devote themselves to, as a form of body chanting (if you will). While priests may have the specialized education in traditional Chinese characters (the canonical language of most Zen scriptures) to copy them from a text or even transcribe them from the recesses of their minds, many people practice *shakyo* by means of tracing the characters with a calligraphy pen on translucent rice paper. Attention here, as in all fine calligraphy practice, is on the focused replication of the characters in proper order (both for the text and the strokes that compose the individual characters) with proper posture, proper moving and breathing (both from the center, or *tanden*), with one exhalation given per character. This unification of form, body, breath, and mind results in a single-pointed focus, that can translate into one's *zazen* practice.

To begin, obtain a translucent piece of paper, such a rice paper or tracing paper, and a paintbrush or a marker. Sit in a comfortable seated position at a table. Lay the paper over the below character from the Heart Sutra for the word Buddha, and begin to trace it. As you do, take deep, focused breaths with each stroke.

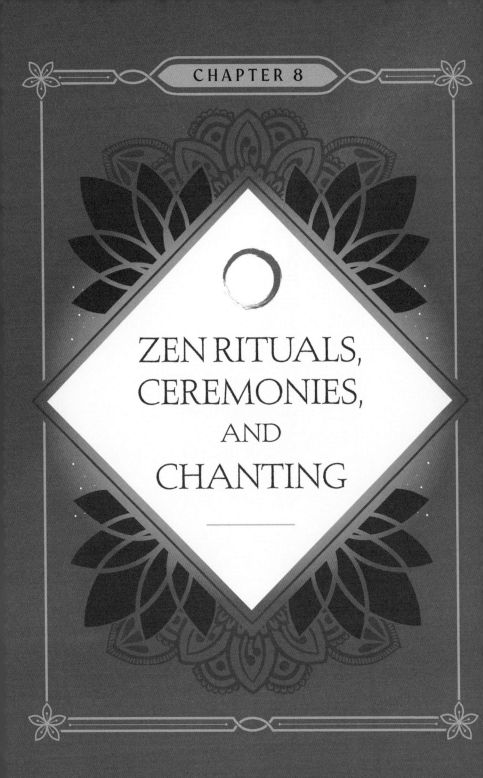

CHAPTER 8

ZEN RITUALS,
CEREMONIES,
AND
CHANTING

I n the postmodern philosophical and religious landscape of
the contemporary global West, nearly since its introduction,
Buddhism has often been the subject of an intense debate: is it a
religion, or a philosophy, or perhaps even less descript, a *way of
life?* Indeed, Buddhism and Zen tend to defy conventional religious
norms that often concern themselves with the pronouncements
of various deities and postmortem rewards for adherence to those
pronouncements. To many, belonging dually to other religious
traditions, Zen is not incompatible, intrinsically, with their beliefs
concerning matter metaphysical. In recent history, a number of
Catholic priests, Jewish rabbis, and many more lay people from
assorted traditions have become duly empowered Zen teachers and
lineage holders, without sacrificing the narratives and metaphors of
their main religious traditions.

Zen seems to be unique in its ability to coexist with other religious traditions and is not a threat to the utility of their cultural containers or dogmas. But, despite its lack of clear congruence with the epistemological rules of religion in the global West, there is no doubt that Zen *is* a religion. It has a parent tradition, which itself was a reform of another world religious movement, it has clergy, scripture, and indeed ritual, ceremony, and liturgy. These latter inclusions are what comprise the focus of this chapter.

RITES, RITUALS, AND LITURGY

While various Zen lineages vary greatly in the amount of ritual, ceremony, and chanting that they include in their practice repertoire, at a minimum most schools will maintain some form of daily chanting, ceremonies for transmitting the precepts (jukai), performing weddings, blessing or welcoming babies, overseeing funerals, ordaining clerics, and transmitting the dharma. Various forms of chanting employed for Buddhist holidays is also common, as are practice forms for prefacing dharma talks or *teisho*, and for opening and closing retreats. Zen Buddhist ceremony generally is divided into three movements:

1. Incense offerings and opening invocations;
2. The recitation of scriptures (sutra), sacred sounds (mantras), and incantations (dharanis); and
3. Well-wishing prayers and dedications of merit.

While the purpose of these rites, rituals, and liturgies can vary in explanation and expectation from center to center and from teacher to teacher, it may be universally understood that they have an effect on the mind that is considered efficacious in the course of Zen Buddhist cultivation and practice.

Chanting (*okyo*) has a complex history in Buddhism, but it is a practice known to almost every religious tradition the world has ever known. While the most obvious historical development with regard to chanting in Buddhism had to do with the Buddha's disciples communally reciting his teachings for the sake of preserving them in the wake of his passing, many scholars posit that early Buddhist practice involved various forms of rhythmic, repetitive verbal recitation as a method of practice in step with the wider religious backdrop from which Buddhism ultimately descended. That said, the chanting of scripture is still an extremely common form of Buddhist practice that, as the preceding chapters have indicated, serves to unify the mind-body of the practitioner with the awakened vision of reality as articulated by the Buddha and successors to his mantle over the past 2,500 years.

It is not uncommon for various Buddhist schools and traditions to chant in canonical languages that are not spoken or necessarily even understood by most practitioners. In these cases, the practice of chanting itself has often been so refined that the mind-body integration demanded by proper form has supplanted the original purpose of chanting, namely as a means of memorizing core teachings before the advent of the printing press.

In its most commonly known iteration in the popular culture of the global West, chanting takes on the form of mantra (a Sanskrit word literally meaning "tool for the mind"), which is in essence a short phrase, often comprised of sacred syllables, that serves to cut through discursive thinking and instill a specific mood or motivation in the practitioner. Usually, Zen teachers assign mantras to students to help them attain clarity, summon energy for practice, and move their minds in a specific direction in relation to their current state of practice. Whereas scriptures or sutras are very frequently chanted and recited in the vernacular language of the practitioners (so they may be conceptually engaged as a form of practice), mantras (like dharanis) are usually left untranslated, so as to not carry or attach to conceptual thought that which could disrupt their assigned intention.

Dharani are much akin to mantras save for the fact that, historically, stemming from their origins in the esoteric practices of the Vedic religions, their focus is often intended outwardly, rather than inwardly, serving then as a place to focus our hopes, longings, and fears. Dharani, like many forms of prayer, provide an outlet for the expression of our innermost anxieties and concerns, and in this as an avenue for catharsis. Prayer and incantation can be understood (and in some circles is) as an actual method to effect outward change, or as a manner to shift the way our inner, idiosyncratic realities interface with the world beyond the bounds of our skin. Following this latter sentiment, we might understand prayer as a manner of excising a metaphorical tumor or growth, with other meditative, dialectical, and scholastic practices forming a treatment regime to arrest the pathology that gave rise to the figurative tumor, and thus its need for excision.

There are yet more subtle aspects to okyo, or chanting, beyond the educational, calibrating, and expressive applications that have been thus far alluded to. One of those primary functions is the embodied, centering effect of proper chanting. Indeed, chanting is not simply an aesthetic practice, it is also an embodiment method that aids practitioners in applying and furthering the breathwork begun in the practice of tanden soku (the diaphragmatic breathing often included in zazen instruction), toward the development of *kiai*. Kiai may be described as the harmonization and unification of one's varied energies into a cohesive, and indeed powerful force that uproots fear, and in its place bridges the heavens with the earth through the dynamic center of the body, the tanden, manifesting a stability and presence that becomes nearly unshakable amidst the various dramas common to life.

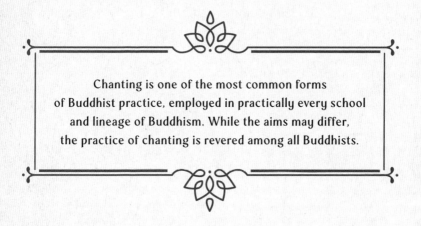

Chanting is one of the most common forms of Buddhist practice, employed in practically every school and lineage of Buddhism. While the aims may differ, the practice of chanting is revered among all Buddhists.

When practiced with the express intent of developing kiai, okyo is performed in the same posture as that employed in zazen and walking meditation practice (*kinhin*), which is to say with the spine upright, the lower abdomen unrestricted, and with the body relaxed and otherwise resting freely on its frame. Okyo is not a practice of simply exercising the vocal cords, but one of opening all of the channels of the body and allowing one's intention and energy to run through them, mindfully metered, as one cohesive unit and process. Proper Zen chanting is initiated in the lower abdomen (tanden), and through the gentle tension and flexing of the abdominal walls air is moved through the belly and sternum, and into the throat where it is directed by the vocal cords and lips to intone the syllables of the chant, be they in English or another canonical Buddhist language. As has already been well established in this text, the mind, body, and breath are deeply interrelated, and by practicing their unification through the intentional engagement with okyo one builds, and otherwise flexes, the firm foundation established in one's sitting practice, electively and mindfully employing it to specific aims, which can expand into every activity. In this, one renders their entire life as practice, and eventually realizes the entire universe as their body, nearing then true shikantaza.

In the pages that follow, a sample daily chanting service will be presented, which can be practiced easily in your home. These verses, scriptures, and prayers should be approached both sincerely and reverently, and though they may be studied and learned from in an academic sense, in the practice of okyo the mind should not be preoccupied with deconstructive or analytical endeavors. Rather, one should strive to simply maintain proper posture, physically and mentally, and to intone each word, syllable by syllable, as a whole expounding of the dharma in its own right. In this way, one may enter into the meditative equilibrium that is to be found in the practice of okyo and not only clear the energetic channels of the body, but also the strictures binding one's life to fear and withdrawal.

Bowing is a gesture as common in East Asia as a handshake is in the West, but bowing has wider usage than mere greeting, and in Buddhist rituals and ceremonies is used to show reverence and to demarcate sacred space and time. Bowing does not necessarily imply deference or worship, but rather invites the body to journey alongside the mind in ritual practice.

In Zen temples and centers, the practice of okyo is usually directed and accompanied by the sounds of various bells, drums, gongs, and claps. The most common of these are the *mokugyo* (a wooden drum shaped like a fish, that is struck in a rhythmic pattern, keeping timing for the chant, syllable by syllable) and the *kesu* (or standing bell, used to signal both starting and stopping points, as well as to add emphasis to passages of chant). None of these are strictly necessary, though if one so desires, they could mimic the mokugyo by gently tapping out a rhythm with something as simple as a pencil on the side of a table. Otherwise, one may just chant with intentionality, precision, and attention, taking time to enunciate each syllable.

In the Japanese style of Zen chanting, very little melody or variability of tone is used in chanting okyo. Certainly, vibrato is all but entirely avoided. The tone should be naturally deep at the lowest natural register of the voice, noting too that the voice should not be unnaturally or unsustainably strained. There is no real melody to speak of in the practice of okyo in its simplest and most straightforward form, there is just full presence and intention, syllable by syllable.

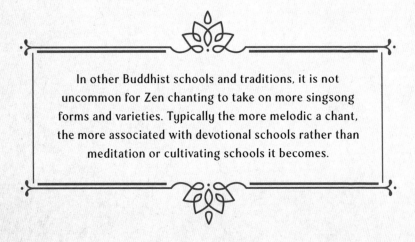

In other Buddhist schools and traditions, it is not uncommon for Zen chanting to take on more singsong forms and varieties. Typically the more melodic a chant, the more associated with devotional schools rather than meditation or cultivating schools it becomes.

DAILY CHANTING SERVICE

VERSE OF THE ROBE

Vast is the robe of liberation,
a formless field of merit garment,
donning the Tathagata's teaching,
to help save all beings

Candles and/or incense may be lit here

INCENSE DEDICATION

Precepts incense, liberation of views incense,
Cloud of lighted incense pouring into the Dharma Realms,
Offering to the highest teachers of the ten directions.
I respectfully bow to the altar of the Incense Cloud Bodhisattva
(repeat the last line three times)

I pray this wonderful incense cloud
will spread out to all the worlds in the ten directions,
as an offering to all the Buddhas and Bodhisattvas,
to the wonderful Dharmas,
to the endless Sravaka assembly,
and to all saints and sages.
I pray it will form an altar of light,
and do the Buddha's work according to its true nature;
benefitting all sentient beings,
so they might arouse Bodhicitta,
depart from evil karma, and attain the highest way

HOMAGE TO THE BUDDHAS

Dharma Master without higher honor,
in three worlds without comparison,
The guiding teacher of nature and man,
father of the four kinds of being,
I now in one thought take refuge,
dissolving three times karma.
Praise and admiration even one hundred thousand kalpas
cannot extinguish.
Namo Shakyamuni Buddha

(repeat last line three times)

PROSTRATIONS

I bow respectfully to all directions of space,
all realms, past, present, and future,
to the ten directions, to all Buddhas,
to the honored Dharma,
and to the enlightened Sangha,
the permanent three treasures.
(bow)

I bow respectfully to the Master of the Samsara world,
our own teacher Sakyamuni Buddha,
to the future coming Maitreya Buddha,
to the Great Love, Great Compassion Amitabha Buddha,
to the Great Compassionate Avalokitesvara Bodhisattva,
to Great Wisdom Manjushri Bodhisattva,
to the Great Vow Kshitigarbha Bodhisattva,
to Great Effort Samantabhadra Bodhisattva,
to the Great Power Mahastamaprapta Bodhisattva,
to the Dharma Protector Bodhisattvas,
and to all Buddhas and Bodhisattvas assembling
at the Great Holy Mountain.
(bow)

I bow respectfully to the principal disciple Venerable Mahakasyapa,
to the wise Venerable Sariputra,
to the pious Venerable Mahamaudgalyana
to the master of the Vinaya Venerable Upali,
to the devoted Dharma guardian Venerable Ananda,
to leader of the Bhikkuni order Venerable Mahaprajapati,
and to all the ancestors of past, present, and future.
(bow)

GOING FOR REFUGE
IN THE TRIPLE GEM

Namô Tassa Bhagavatô Arahatô Sammâ-Sambuddhassa
(repeat above line two times)
Homage to the Fully Awakened, Perfectly Enlightened Buddha

Buddham Saranam Gacchâmi.

Dhammam Saranam Gacchâmi.

Sangham Saranam Gacchâmi.

(repeat each line twice)

I take refuge in the Buddha,
I take refuge in the Dharma,
I take refuge in the Sangha

DAILY CONFESSION

I respectfully bow to Śākyamuni Buddha,
Amitābha Buddha, all Buddhas in the ten directions,
boundless Buddha-Dharma,
and the virtuous Sangha.
Having lived many lives,
under heavy karmic obstacles:
desire, anger, pride, illusion, and ignorance;
today because of Buddha's teaching, knowing this as mistake,
with sincere heart I confess.
I vow to eliminate evils, and to do good,
I respectfully entreat the Buddhas for their compassionate assistance:
body without sickness, mind empty of frustration and anxiety.
Every day happy to practice the wonderful teaching of the Buddha
in order to quickly depart from birth and death,
understand mind, seeing into its true nature,
develop wisdom and gain the spiritual power;
in order to rescue all of my honored elders,
fathers, mothers, brothers, sisters, friends, relatives,
and may all living beings attain complete Buddhahood.

SUTRA OPENING VERSE

The unsurpassed, deep, profound, subtle, and wonderful Dharma,
which is difficult to encounter even in countless kalpas,
coming now to receive and behold it with both sight and sound,
I vow to realize its true and actual meaning.

THE HEART SUTRA

Avalokitesvara Bodhisattva
when practicing deeply the Prajna Paramita
perceives that all five skandhas are empty
and is saved from all suffering and distress.
Shariputra, form does not differ from emptiness,
emptiness does not differ from form.
That which is form is emptiness, that which is emptiness form.
The same is true of feelings, perceptions, impulses, and consciousness.
Shariputra, all dharmas are marked with emptiness;
they do not appear or disappear,
are not tainted or pure,
do not increase or decrease.

Therefore, in emptiness there is no form,
no feelings, perceptions, impulses, or consciousness.
No eyes, no ears, no nose, no tongue, no body, no mind;
no color, no sound, no smell, no taste, no touch, no object of mind;
no realm of eyes and so forth until no realm of mind consciousness.
No ignorance and also no extinction of it,
and so forth until no old age and death and also no extinction of them.
No suffering, no origination, no stopping, no path, no cognition,
also no attainment with nothing to attain.
The Bodhisattva depends on Prajna Paramita and the mind
is no hindrance;
without any hindrance no fears exist.
Far apart from every perverted view one dwells in Nirvana.
In the three worlds all Buddhas depend on Prajna Paramita
and attain Anuttara Samyak Sambodhi.
Therefore know that Prajna Paramita is the great transcendent mantra,
is the great bright mantra, is the utmost mantra, is the supreme mantra
which is able to relieve all suffering and is true, not false.
So proclaim the Prajna Paramita mantra,
proclaim the mantra which says:
gate gate paragate parasamgate bodhi svaha
(Repeat last line three times)

*A period of seated meditation practice is appropriate here,
before resuming chanting.*

BUDDHA'S NAME RECITATION

Namo Shakyamuni Buddha
Namo Amitabha Buddha
Namo Chundi Bodhisattva
(repeat each line fifteen times individually)

BODHISATTVA VOWS

Sentient beings are numberless, I vow to save them all.
Delusions are endless, I vow to cut through them all.
The teachings are infinite, I vow to learn them all.
The Buddha way is inconceivable, I vow to realize it.

WELL-WISHING PRAYER

May the suffering ones be suffering free,
and the fear-struck, fearless be.
May the grieving shed all grief,
and the sick find health-relief.

DEDICATION OF MERIT

I wish that all this merit
Be extended to everyone
That we, together with all beings
May gain the Buddha's Way
(repeat the entire verse three times)

*Three closing bows may be offered here,
and any candles or incense may be extinguished.*

Note that, out of necessity, many Zen practices are often given without seemingly sufficient instruction. The general feeling of the Zen tradition is that practice should first be experienced, and from experience can grow understanding. The daily service outlined in the preceding pages contains enough bounding places for research to last an entire lifetime, and while understanding each of these facets, and being able to articulate that understanding as part of a unified religious theory is a laudable thing, one must be careful to not be derailed in their practice and miss the forest for the trees, as idiomatic wisdom cautions. Always endeavor first to authentically capture the feeling of the practice, and everything else will fall into alignment. This is perhaps the only matter of faith in the practice of Zen Buddhism— trust the process!

In Zen, chanting is a unique practice path, not simply a devotional activity unto itself. When chanting one should try their utmost to "become one" with the activity at hand, allowing the body, mind, and breath to unify in meditative absorption, and allow any extraneous thinking to fall away.

In chanting properly executed, one enters into the realm of the teachings themselves, allowing their mind to become as a channel for the organic and pure expression of *Buddha Dharma*. In this way, the teachings bypass the gates of cognition and become manifest in one's actions and very being, and for that time, one becomes nondifferent from the Buddhas and awakened ancestors.

In this, chanting is not just a common manner of memorizing teachings, or of affective performance, or even of normative cultivation, but properly engaged, chanting and liturgy are manners of stepping into the epitome of awakening in this very life and moment. In this place, one can pick up on the feeling and flavor of enlightenment and carry its scent into their daily lives and schedules.

It has been said that the efficacious cultivation of awakening is a bit like swooping down from above, while climbing up from below. Meditation may be considered a mode of climbing up from below, and chanting may be considered a method of swooping down from above. Just as it is quicker to fly from one locale to another than it is to drive, in some real sense the process of dropping into Buddhahood in chanting is more efficient than realizing it organically in silent contemplation. The most expeditious and integrative method of realization, then, is the concurrent pursuit of both methods—shoring up the ground while soaring through the skies.

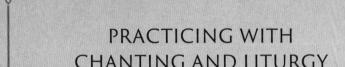

PRACTICING WITH
CHANTING AND LITURGY

As a final addition to your daily Zen Buddhist practice routine, we will now explore the practice of chanting. Earlier in this chapter, a sample daily chanting liturgy has been clearly spelled out. Ideally, one would begin daily practice with chanting the daily service (which can take between 5 and 10 minutes when mindfully engaged), followed by at least 10 minutes of meditation practice, and 10 minutes of study into the scriptures and commentaries on the tradition. Following these three practices will build a daily schedule of around 30 minutes, which is the minimum that most sincere Zen Buddhist practitioners commit to fitting into their schedules in pursuit of liberation and awakening.

- As outlined in this chapter, chanting should be done as a meditative practice, with proper posture, and bodily alignment so that air can be moved from the lower abdomen through the vocal cords.

- Chanting in the Japanese Zen tradition is typically done in a lower register than speaking, but not in a forced or harsh tone, and should be done in a volume slightly louder than speaking conversationally.

- Each syllable should be mindfully pronounced, and tapping on a table or floor, or small drum of some sort can accompany each syllable to keep the pace and invite the body fully into the practice.

It's important not to rush your chanting practice, as a primary function of chanting is to cut through discursive thinking, while adding the wisdom of the liturgy into one's consciousness, with daily attunement through practice so that the wisdom of the liturgy may be made manifest in one's life, through the eventual attainment of unconscious competence.

It can be helpful to seek out online resources for examples of how Zen chanting services are typically done, which can serve as a bounding point for emulation for solo practitioners.

Chanting should be practiced routinely, and it need not continually grow to encompass an endless number of texts or scriptures.

Gaining familiarity with the basic teachings and commitments of Zen practice, over familiarity even, is essential.

Remember, boredom is a privilege afforded to those with the time to return to the very simple processes of Zen over and over again. Approaching boredom with intentionality is a key practice in support of gaining the agency that is required to advance in understanding and realization alike.

Approach each moment, each line, and each syllable of your chanting practice as if it were anew, even if being recited purely from memory.

CONCLUSION

Having now broadly explored the history and development of Buddhism, the key teachings of the Zen tradition specifically, the place of spiritual guides and teachers within Zen, life by vow and the practice of precepts, Zen's methods of meditation, the place of study and scholasticism on the spiritual path, Zen rituals, ceremonies, and chanting you have no doubt been thoroughly introduced to a relatively full portrait of what a life engaged in Zen practice could entail. Every effort has been taken in the writing of this text to avoid the extraordinary promises and often exclusionary claims that befall most religious traditions in their self-reflection, and still, poetry is all but guaranteed in attempting to describe the transformation of life through the practice of profound attention given to both its contents and one's presuppositions.

Zen promises freedom, and for a great many sincere practitioners it has delivered in fuller ways than can even be imagined. The cost, though, is not insignificant. The Zen path is not one of clear, linear progression. It is fundamentally a deconstructive path that takes away more than it adds on. It demands nothing less than sincere devotion, persistence, and long suffering. Wise teachers and spiritual friends (sangha) are essential for success. While the path is ultimately one of personal, solitary endeavor, the efficaciousness of the balm that is being alone together in this endeavor (before inevitably coming to realize that it's never been possible to be apart from anyone or anything for even a moment) cannot be emphasized enough.

If after reading this book you find that your life has been enriched by a new perspective or two, but that is all of the interest that you have in Zen at this time, there is nothing wrong with that. You've planted the karmic seeds for the ongoing sprouting of your own wellbeing, and that is certainly enough! If, though, you find yourself somewhat enticed or even haunted by Zen's vision of awakened reality, it is essential that you find a competent guide to journey with you on this path (reviewing chapter three is advised). The path that awaits you, be it long or short, quick or prolonged, is sure to be the road trip of a lifetime. Keep your eyes on the road, but don't neglect the horizon; mind the maps and the rumble strips, and share the driving whenever possible.

There are innumerable resources now published in print and online in the English language, written by and for Western practitioners. It would be wise to peruse at least several more beyond the present text so that a fuller glimpse of the feeling and character of the Zen way might be deduced in sorting through a number of voices and perspectives.

May you be happy, may you be well, may you be free from suffering, and from the causes of suffering, may all good come to you, and may you persist in this world with peace and ease, regardless of the path that lies ahead.

INDEX

D

E

F

G

H

J

T

V

ABOUT THE AUTHOR

The Rev. Dr. Joshua Richard Paszkiewicz (*in ecclesia the Most Venerable Sunyananda Dharmacarya*) is a priest, Zen teacher, psychotherapist, martial artist, healer, culinarian, writer, academic, and mystic.

A multi-yana trained, fully authorized Zen teacher, Dr. Paszkiewicz is the only individual to hold full, simultaneous teaching authority in the Japanese, Korean, and Vietnamese Zen schools. Dr. Paszkiewicz has studied and taught Buddhism throughout the world, lectured at numerous colleges and universities, and has appeared in and written for various media outlets, in addition to serving as an official delegate to numerous notable Buddhist events, including the first White House Buddhist Leaders Conference, and the United Nations World Day of Vesak.

On a day-to-day basis Dr. Paszkiewicz serves as the headmaster of the Blue Dragon Order, a religious order of Zen Priests scattered throughout the country, and as rector of its seminary and formation program, The Zen School.

First published in 2023 by Wellfleet, an imprint of The Quarto Group,
142 West 36th Street, 4th Floor, New York, NY 10018, USA
T (212) 779-4972 F (212) 779-6058 www.Quarto.com

Wellfleet titles are also available at discount for retail, wholesale, promotional, and bulk
purchase. For details, contact the Special Sales Manager by email at specialsales@quarto.com
or by mail at The Quarto Group, Attn: Special Sales Manager, 100 Cummings Center Suite
265D, Beverly, MA 01915 USA.

10 9 8 7 6 5 4 3 2

ISBN: 978-1-57715-365-8

Library of Congress Cataloging-in-Publication Data

Names: Paszkiewicz, Joshua R., author.
Title: Zen Buddhism : your personal guide to practice and tradition / Joshua R. Paszkiewicz.
Description: New York : Wellfleet Press, 2023. | Series: Mystic traditions
   ; 1 | Summary: "Zen Buddhism is the perfect addition to your spiritual
   journey and a great way to strengthen your Zen"-- Provided by publisher.
Identifiers: LCCN 2022046250 (print) | LCCN 2022046251 (ebook) | ISBN
   9781577153658 (hardcover) | ISBN 9780760382233 (ebook)
Subjects: LCSH: Zen Buddhism. | Buddhism.
Classification: LCC BQ9266 .P379 2023 (print) | LCC BQ9266 (ebook) | DDC
   294.3/927--dc23/eng/20221004
LC record available at https://lccn.loc.gov/2022046250
LC ebook record available at https://lccn.loc.gov/2022046251

Publisher: Rage Kindelsperger
Creative Director: Laura Drew
Managing Editor: Cara Donaldson
Editor: Sara Bonacum
Cover and Interior Design: Amelia LeBarron

Printed in China